PRAISE FOR *SINK THEN SWIM*

"*Sink Then Swim* made me reevaluate how I view and handle change in my own life. It provides essential tools for understanding all types of change and includes valuable swimming lessons to deal with both events and emotions. I especially love the insights on how to turn difficult emotions upside down. *Sink Then Swim* is a real lifesaver."

Agnes Bamford
Researcher and Lecturer at the Norwegian School of Economics and Intercultural Trainer and Business Coach at Culture-lens, https://culture-lens.com
Author of Swings and Roundabouts: A Self-Coaching Workbook for Parents and Those Considering Becoming Parents

"*Sink Then Swim* is a practical guide for anyone living abroad. Sue Schoormans' personal anecdotes – like overcoming fear of drowning by finding rhythm and gliding effortlessly in deeper waters – are blended with actionable advice. This metaphor of resilience and self-trust symbolizes thriving in turbulent times, making the book an invaluable resource for navigating challenges abroad."

Anastasia Aldelina Lijadi, PhD
Psychologist and gender equity enthusiast at the International Institute for Applied Systems Analysis, Austria, and Vice President of Families in Global Transition.
https://iiasa.ac.at/staff/anastasia-aldelina-lijadi

"If you're living abroad, keep this book close by! It might just be the secret toolkit that saves you from endless sleepless nights and marathon sessions of overthinking. Personally, the chapters 'Navigating Culture' and 'Preparing for the Worst' spoke to my soul. The practical, no-nonsense tips are a breath of fresh air, and the swimming lessons are so good, you'll actually want to fill them out (no, really!)."

Andrea Schmitt Lozano
Life Coach for Teen Girls, Host of the TCK Research Podcast and TEDx Speaker.
https://www.globalgirlcoach.com

"A deeply insightful and enriching exploration of how to navigate life's most challenging moments while living abroad. Through real-life stories and practical exercises, the author invites readers to reflect on this unique journey of transformation – one that challenges, but also illuminates, our values, beliefs, and sense of identity. Thoughtful, pragmatic, with a touch of unexpected wit!"

Camilla Celati
International C-Suite Executive Coach, Senior Leadership Advisor and Cross-Cultural Leadership Expert. www.CamillaCelati.com

"*Sink Then Swim* is an honest, practical, and deeply human guide to navigating life abroad. Sue Schoormans blends personal stories with grounded reflection to help readers face emotional upheaval with clarity and resilience. It is a refreshingly real book for anyone tackling change, culture shock, or adversity in a foreign land."

Chris Schutte
Managing Director at InterACT-Global. www.interact-global.co

"Sue Schoormans is a warm, wise and wonderful coach and trainer who has the unique ability to make the complex simple. This book is a great illustration of her skill."

Damian Hughes
Sunday Times best-selling Author, Trusted Advisor to elite coaches and co-host of The High Performance Podcast. His latest book is High Performance: Lessons from the Best on Becoming Your Best. www.liquidthinker.com

"I loved reading *Sink Then Swim*. It's a real gem for expat life, loaded with reflection exercises that are super helpful for anyone – not just those living abroad. Sue Schoormans' structured approach with heartfelt, real-life stories and a focus on values, strengths and self leadership makes this book a valuable resource. As a former HR Director I wish I'd had this guide when supporting international colleagues."

Dorothy Matthew
Founder of Brilliant People Consulting. https://brilliant-people.co.uk

"From now on, every expat will be able to first sink and then swim when entering new waters. This personal, moving and practical self-help book guides expats in managing common challenges with the right swimming lessons, a touch of British humour and many practical tips from those who travelled the road before, including the author's. A rewarding read and a life-saver!"

Esther Janssen
Managing Director at Culture-Inc. Speaker and Author of Zakendoen van hier tot Tokio: slagen of falen bij cultuurverschillen.
https://www.culture-inc.com

"Sue Schoormans' resilience in overcoming her struggles shines through in this book – a book filled with inspiring real-life stories and practical tips. Whether you're currently living abroad, or soon will be, you'll get the guidance you need so that you can confidently swim in foreign seas."

Greta Solomon
Freelance Journalist and Author of Heart, Sass & Soul (Mango, 2019).
www.gretasolomon.com

"*Sink Then Swim* offers valuable insights through diverse relocation stories alongside the author's personal experiences. Sue Schoormans masterfully combines practical advice with emotional wisdom, showing how to navigate life's challenges abroad – from cultural adjustment to personal loss. The structured approach with swimming lessons and practical tools empowers readers to not just survive difficulties but emerge stronger. Highly recommended for anyone facing change."

Kristin Miai Birkeland
Global Talent Acquisition Partner at Norges Bank Investment Management

"*Sink Then Swim* is a refreshingly easy-to-read guide for navigating life challenges that may arise when living abroad. Through real stories, it helps you ride the waves of change and feel comfortable with the uncomfortable. For anyone preparing to or who has already jumped into a new life abroad, this guide is a life raft worth grabbing."

Nathalie Owe
Key Account Manager at Santa Fe Relocation

"*Sink Then Swim* shares personal stories that you will be able to relate to when living abroad and help you turn your own experiences into learning, transformation, self-awareness and self-confidence."

Pauline Vromans
Learning Designer and Lecturer at the University of Amsterdam and Intercultural Trainer at Intercultural Minds. www.interculturalminds.com

"Life's challenges are always hard to face. And as I started reading Sue Schoormans' book, I wasn't sure I wanted to face any of mine, past, present or future. But through the stories and swimming lessons, I was reminded that I have strengths and people who walk alongside me to draw on at all times."

Rhoda Bangerter
Split Family Assignments Specialist and Author of Holding the Fort Abroad.
www.rhodabangerter.com

"Reading *Sink Then Swim* was an experience of reflection, inspiration and recognition. Having lived in several countries, I found comfort reading stories like my own and acknowledging not being alone during these challenges. This book not only provides practical guidance through personal stories demonstrating resilience, exercises and tips but also gives a message of hope – life abroad may not be easy but it is an opportunity from which to learn and grow. Highly recommended."

Romee Rutgers van der Loeff
Vice President HR at Circana

"Exploring the challenges of living abroad head-on, *Sink Then Swim* is a must-read for anyone considering relocating or having already done so. Sue Schoormans navigates these challenges with practical steps and tips from those who know, doesn't shy away from the lows or the highs, using meaningful stories, and uses a touch of humour along the way."

Tara Lloyd
Head of HR EMEA

SINK THEN SWIM

How to survive life's most stressful situations when living abroad

Sue Schoormans

Springtime Books
Bringing Your Book to Life

First published in Great Britain by Springtime Books 2025

Copyright © Sue Schoormans 2025

All rights reserved. No part of this publication may be reproduced, stored in or introduced into a retrieval system, or transmitted, in any form, or by any means (electronic, mechanical, photocopying recording or otherwise) without the prior written permission of the publisher.

This book is sold subject to the condition that it shall not, by way of trade or otherwise, be lent, resold, hired out, or otherwise circulated without the publisher's prior consent in any form of binding or cover other than that in which it is published and without a similar condition including this condition being imposed on the subsequent purchaser.

ISBN: 978-1-915548-21-4

Every effort has been made to contact owners of copyrighted materials referenced in this book for permission to use such materials.

Disclaimer

The author of this book is not a medical expert, psychologist or solicitor. This book contains opinions, thoughts and beliefs and is not a replacement for medical or legal advice.

Some names, locations and identifying features of people in the stories have been changed to preserve their anonymity.

Mountaineer, explorer and anthropologist Sir Edmund Hilary once said, "It is not the mountain we conquer, but ourselves." He and fellow mountaineer Tenzing Norgay were the first to reach the summit of Mount Everest.

This book is dedicated to you. You are the one who, when facing any of life's most stressful situations when living abroad, will not only survive but will conquer yourself in the process.

CONTENTS

Foreword xiii

INTRODUCTION 1

PART ONE – WAVE UPON WAVE OF CHANGE

Chapter One – Calm Choppy Waters 9
Sink or Swim? 9
You Are No Stranger to Change 12
Change in Our Wider World 13
Change in Your World 16
Swimming Lesson One – Major Changes in Your Life 18
Why Change Is Difficult 19
Thoughts and Emotions 19
Swimming Lesson Two – Change and Your Emotions 26
Be Confident, Be Calm, Gain Clarity, Benefit from Connections and Embrace Happiness 27
Chapter Summary 27

Chapter Two – Navigating Culture 29
The Globalisation Conundrum 29
Above and Below the Surface of the Water 32
Swimming Lesson Three – Cultural Similarities and Differences 33
Cultural Waves 35
Swimming Lesson Four – From One Cultural Wave to Another 37
Chapter Summary 39

PART TWO – DIVE DEEP INTO WHO YOU REALLY ARE

Chapter Three – Crystal Clear Waters: Your Values 43
What Are Values? 43
From Where Do Values Originate? 44
Values Fluctuate 45

Values Matter   46
Swimming Lesson Five – Realise Your Values 🏊 49
Chapter Summary   59

Chapter Four – Swimming Strokes: Your Strengths   61
What Are Strengths?   61
From Where Do Strengths Originate?   62
Strengths Fluctuate   63
Strengths Matter   64
Swimming Lesson Six – Realise Your Strengths 🏊 66
Not Forgetting Weaknesses   76
Swimming Lesson Seven – Strengths to Overcome Weaknesses 🏊 77
Chapter Summary   79

PART THREE – SINK THEN SWIM DURING LIFE'S MOST STRESSFUL SITUATIONS

Chapter Five – Sink Then Swim Living Abroad: The Stories   83
The Foundation of Your Life Abroad   83
1. Where's Home? Anna's Living Abroad Story   86
2. It's the Small Things That Matter: Evgeny's Living Abroad Story   90
3. Unwrap the *Why* of Your Host Country's Culture: Hortense's Living Abroad Story   94
4. Parallel Tracks: Laura's Living Abroad Story   98
5. Missing Out: Matilde's Living Abroad Story   102
6. On a Journey Doing the Best You Can: Nicole's Living Abroad Story   106
7. Pay It Forward: Pauline's Living Abroad Story   110

Swimming Lesson Eight – Living Abroad 🏊 114
Chapter Summary   115

Chapter Six – Preparing for the Worst: Death of a Relative   119
No Weddings, Just Funerals   119
Calling to Say Goodbye – Anna's Story: Death of a Relative   120
Champagne and Bracelets – Pauline's Story: Death of Two Relatives   124
Anna and Pauline's Tips – Death of a Relative   129
Swimming Lesson Nine – Death of a Relative 🏊 131
Chapter Summary   132

Chapter Seven – Storms Don't Last Forever: Divorce and Separation 135
Has Our Ship Sailed? 135
Whirlwind Romances Are Awesome but Sometimes Shit Happens – Nicole's Story: Divorce 137
Third Time Lucky? – Laura's Story: Separation 141
Nicole and Laura's Tips – Divorce and Separation 146
Swimming Lesson Ten – Divorce and Separation 🏊 148
Chapter Summary 150

Chapter Eight – Dealing With the Unthinkable: Ill-Health 153
Living a Nightmare 153
Find the Best Way to Be Present – Matilde's Story: Ill-Health 154
Heal from the Inside Out – My Story: Ill-Health 158
Tips from Matilde and Me – Ill-Health 163
Swimming Lesson Eleven – Ill-Health 🏊 165
Chapter Summary 166

Chapter Nine – In Turbulent Waters: Finding a Job 169
When One Boat Sails Another One Docks 169
Looking for a Job Is a Job in Itself – Evgeny's Story: Finding a Job 170
Starting From Zero – Hortense's Story: Finding a Job 174
Evgeny and Hortense's Tips – Finding a Job 178
Swimming Lesson Twelve – Finding a Job 🏊 180
Chapter Summary 181

PART FOUR – ON THE CREST OF A WAVE

Chapter Ten – Mastering Swimming Strokes: Developing Values and Strengths 185
Gain Even More Confidence, Calmness, Clarity, Connections and Happiness 185
Defining and Developing Values and Strengths 186
Adaptability 189
Connections 191
Courage 193
Humour 195
Integrity 197
Listening Skills 199

Observation Skills   201
Perseverance   203
Pragmatism   205
Questioning Skills   207
Resilience   210
Willingness to Learn   213
Swimming Lesson Thirteen – Developing Your Values and Strengths 🏊   215
Chapter Summary   224

Chapter Eleven – Be a Shellfish? Nope, Be Selfish   225
Self-Leadership   225
Self-Awareness – I Am ...   226
Self-Belief – I Can ...   228
Self-Confidence – I Am ... and I Can ...   229
Swimming Lesson Fourteen – Get Selfish 🏊   232
Reward Yourself   237
First You Sink and Then You Swim   238
The Six Steps to Swimming Again   239
Swimming Lesson Fifteen – The Six Steps to Swimming Again 🏊   240
Chapter Summary   242

Sue's Final Message   245
Bibliography   247
Acknowledgements   249
About the Author   251

FOREWORD

Sink Then Swim is more than a book; it's a lifeline. Writing from the heart and drawing on a lifetime of experience, Sue has created something truly special: a guide, a companion and a source of comfort for anyone navigating life abroad.

Living abroad has many blessings, but it can also come with deep emotional, practical and psychological challenges. Sue doesn't shy away from this truth. Instead, she meets it with courage, empathy and wisdom. This book explores how to cope with, and even grow through, life's most stressful situations abroad, from the death of a loved one to divorce, separation, illness, job loss, and so much more.

Sink Then Swim is comprehensive and relatable. The clarity of each chapter, the thoughtful exercises, and the resources offered at the end provide not only insight but also action – tools to help readers find their footing when everything feels uncertain.

I especially appreciate the inclusion of stories of those living abroad. These real-life narratives offer comfort, perspective and valuable lessons, showing readers that others have walked this path too. Reading Sue's own timeline of significant life events deeply moved me. It's rare to see such honesty and vulnerability on the page.

Sue also skilfully blends personal reflection, science and practical knowledge. She brings in core concepts like self-leadership, values and strengths – not as abstract ideas, but as essential lifelines when navigating change and loss. This balance of heart and head is one of the book's greatest strengths.

This isn't just another expat book about life abroad… it's Sue's life project. Her lived wisdom fills every chapter and this authenticity makes it deeply impactful. Through her words, she teaches us how to swim when we're drowning, how to come up for air, and eventually reach the shore.

It gave me food for thought, it taught me a lot, and most importantly, it made me feel less alone. I highly recommend *Sink Then Swim* to anyone living an international life, whether you're just beginning or deep in the waves. In pouring her experience and insight into these pages, Sue has given us a book we can turn to when everything feels uncertain, as well as a steady compass to help us find direction so we can thrive again.

Vivian Chiona, Director and Founder of Expat Nest
www.expatnest.com

INTRODUCTION

"No one ever said your life would be easy. The nature of being human makes life for all of us a challenge. The most important thing to consider here is this. Your life is only as challenging as you think it is. Think of a challenge as a teacher and yourself the student. It's up to you to figure out what the lesson is to be learned. To learn that lesson and build the strength and courage to face other challenges."

James A Murphy
Author and licensed and certified practitioner in neuro-linguistic and strategic intervention coaching

You are about to embark on a journey of learning How to Survive Life's Most Stressful Situations When Living Abroad.

Let's get started.

Why I Wrote This Book

"One day you will tell your story of how you've overcome what you are going through now, and it will become part of someone else's survival guide." American professor and writer Brené Brown's quote is precisely why I wrote this book. Having experienced three of what I class as the top four most stressful situations in life, namely, death of a relative, divorce and separation, ill-health and finding a job, I had, as the idiom says, 'Been there, done that and got the t-shirt'. It was time to put pen to paper.

So, here is my first book, *Sink Then Swim: How to Survive Life's Most Stressful Situations When Living Abroad*. My hope is it will become your go-to survival guide for dealing with these situations and others like them.

Why You Should Read This Book

This book has been written with you in mind. You are:

- An expat, immigrant, asylum seeker, refugee or international student living abroad or planning to do so.
- Repatriating to or living in your home country following a period of living abroad.
- Currently coping with the death of a relative, divorce or separation, ill-health or finding a job.
- Seeking to comprehend how to handle life's most stressful situations because you recognise you will likely need to manage one or more of these during your time abroad.
- Searching for practical, step-by-step information and easy-to-implement tools and techniques to assist you in managing life's most stressful situations when living abroad.
- Aspiring to be your authentic self, knowing this will make you better equipped to survive life's most stressful situations when living abroad.

When you have finished reading this book, you will have both the know-how and confidence to survive life's most stressful situations when living abroad.

How to Use This Book

The best way to take the learnings from this book is to read it in order, cover to cover. You may then decide to revisit specific chapters and further explore certain topics – to make the learning stick. Alternatively, you may decide to dip in and out of one or more chapters. Be aware, however, that by not reading the book in its entirety, you will miss out on some of the learnings.

Almost all chapters contain stories, a *swimming lesson* or two and a chapter summary. Let's take a look at each of these in turn.

Stories

People love to read stories. They are great teachers, illustrating one or more points in a memorable way. For this reason, stories form a significant part of this book.

INTRODUCTION

I instinctively knew that the best way to acquire information for the stories was to conduct semi-structured interviews. These conversation-like interviews involved asking pre-prepared questions and then probing certain answers, digging deeper to gain clarity. Two themes were explored: living abroad and life's most stressful situations. The information obtained gave great insight into each of the themes.

Note: Pseudonyms have been used and some identifying features changed where interviewees wished to remain anonymous.

Swimming Lessons

There's an old Chinese proverb, 'Tell me and I will forget, show me and I may remember, involve me and I will understand'. Each chapter in this book contains one or two *Swimming Lessons* providing you with the opportunity to reflect upon and solidify what you have learned and to apply the learning in your life. I recommend you:

- Complete every lesson.
- Write your answers in the spaces provided. If you would rather keep your book free from notes and scribbles or are reading this in e-book format, however, I recommend using a separate notebook or typing your answers on a PC or tablet.
- When completing the lessons:
  - Read each question carefully and reflect on what you are being asked to do. Don't rush. It's not a race.
  - Set aside the recommended time.
- Move on if you get stuck or are unable to complete the lesson, but feel free to return to the lesson later.
- Take the *Swimming Lessons* more than once. You will discover new things and your confidence will grow.

Journaling

Some of the *Swimming Lessons* require you to journal. Journaling involves documenting your thoughts, emotions, reflections, insights, ideas, observations and experiences. When you journal, you embark on a journey of self-discovery and self-improvement.

To help you get started, I suggest you:

- Buy a notebook and use it purely for journaling.
- Write, draw, or combine the two, perhaps by using mind mapping.
- Let your pen do the talking. Don't think about what you intend to write. Just write. Go with the flow.

Chapter Summaries

At the end of each chapter, you'll find a summary comprising:

- Chapter learnings.
- Additional recommended resources, including books and videos.
- Jokes. There's no getting away from it; the subject of this book is rather serious. For this very reason, jokes titled *A Ripple of Laughter* appear at the end of each chapter. Humour, after all, is a great way to get through life's challenges.

This Is Your Book

Make this book your own. Write in it. Underline key messages. Do what feels right for you.

What Is This Book About?

Sink Then Swim explains How to Survive Life's Most Stressful Situations When Living Abroad. Organised in four parts, it contains eleven chapters, each building on the previous, except for the chapters in *PART THREE*, which stand alone.

PART ONE, titled *Wave Upon Wave of Change*, shines a spotlight on the subject of change. *Chapter One, Calm Choppy Waters*, seeks to unravel whether change is difficult and if so why. *Chapter Two, Navigating Culture*, considers the extent to which we live in a global world. Homing in on culture, the integration journey and culture shock are discussed.

Unpacking what makes you you forms the content of *PART TWO, Dive Deep Into Who You Really Are*. In *Chapter Three, Crystal Clear Waters – Your Values*, the subject of values is addressed. After defining values and looking at where they originate from, whether they change over time and why they matter, you'll unpack your own values. *Chapter Four, Swimming Strokes – Your Strengths*, delves into the subject of strengths. After answering what they are, where they originate from, whether they fluctuate, why they matter and how they can compensate for weaknesses, you'll realise your own strengths.

PART THREE, Sink Then Swim During Life's Most Stressful Situations, features stories about life abroad and stories covering death, divorce and separation, ill-health and finding a job when living abroad. Sharing the experiences of people living abroad, *Chapter Five, Sink Then Swim Living Abroad – The Stories*, looks at the circumstances in which people sank and then swam, what they learned on their integration journey and which of their values and strengths surfaced when managing their lives abroad. *Chapter Six, Preparing for the Worst – Death of a Relative*, reveals how Anna and Pauline dealt with the death of one or more relatives. *Chapter Seven, Storms Don't Last Forever – Divorce and Separation*, looks at how Nicole and Laura worked through divorce and separation. In *Chapter Eight, Dealing With the Unthinkable – Ill-Health*, Matilde and I divulge how we handled ill-health. *Chapter Nine, In Turbulent Waters – Finding a Job*, features Evgeny's and Hortense's experiences of finding work.

PART FOUR, titled *On the Crest of a Wave*, unveils how to become the successful leader of your life abroad and how important this is. *Chapter Ten, Mastering Swimming Strokes – Developing Values and Strengths*, defines the values and strengths highlighted in *Chapter Five* and details ways in which these can be developed as your own. *Chapter Eleven, Be a Shellfish? Nope, Be Selfish*, explores the ABC of self and why this is important. Finally, The Six Steps to Swimming Again toolkit is unveiled.

Before You Start

Be Your Own Advocate

This book contains my opinions, thoughts and beliefs. What you read is not a replacement for medical or legal advice. I am not a medical expert, psychologist or solicitor. I therefore recommend that when you need advice, support or assistance, you reach out to a qualified and experienced professional. You are responsible for how you use the information in this book. *Be your own advocate.*

Emotions

Let's be honest, dealing with the death of a relative, divorce or separation, ill-health or finding a job may well bring about one or more emotional reactions. And when you read the related stories in this book, you may encounter the same, laughing one minute and crying the next. The objective of this book is not to dive into the understanding of emotional states but instead to focus on how you can best manage these while dealing with life's most stressful situations when living abroad.

Repetition

"Tell them what you are going to tell them, tell them, and then tell them what you told them." This quote from Aristotle highlights the importance of repetition. My goal is for you to learn How to Survive Life's Most Stressful Situations When Living Abroad, and because learning can take time, you'll find some repetition within this book.

Get In Touch

I'd love to hear from you when you've finished reading. What worked for you? Which sections of the book were the most useful? What else did you discover about yourself? Any feedback, suggestions or questions you may have are most welcome. You can get in touch with me here:

www.sueschoormansauthor.com

PART ONE
WAVE UPON WAVE OF CHANGE

> "Change will force you to step off the path, to venture from the nest, to close your eyes and dive right in, knowing that the greatest opportunities in life are found in the sink or swim, do or die moments."

Stella Payton
American author, speaker and
CEO of Making People Priority Consulting Group

CHAPTER ONE
Calm Choppy Waters

"You can't stop the waves, but you can learn to surf."

Jon Kabat-Zinn
American professor and pioneer of Mindfulness

Sink or Swim?

Sink or swim? Is this the only choice you have to manage change when living abroad?

The Netherlands, January 2022

With tears rolling down my cheeks, I turned to Hans.

"I can't do this. I have no strength to deal with this."

Just over an hour earlier, having walked down what seemed to be the longest hospital corridor ever, we had been greeted by not one but two medical professionals. This isn't good, I remember thinking to myself. Upon entering the doctor's office, we were told the cancer had returned. I would be facing six months of intensive treatment – chemotherapy, breast removal and radiotherapy.

"We'll blast this thing," one of the doctors said.

In a state of complete disbelief, I remembered nothing more of what was said.

This was never meant to happen. That chapter was closed. For five years I had not once believed the cancer would return.

There were no words, and had there been, I couldn't have expressed the anguish I was experiencing. The grip around my throat was too tight.

Sink or swim?

Swept away in the deepest and darkest of choppy waters, I was sinking at a rate of knots.

The days and nights that followed were unsettling to the point of being alarming. Heavy thoughts and emotions debilitated my body. Most days involved lying on the sofa staring into nowhere, and most nights were awash with disturbing nightmares. Seeing my coffin in a hearse outside our home is by far the worst nightmare I've ever had. When I woke up, I believed my time was up. Death was knocking at the door.

I was in an unpleasant place, and unbeknown to me, things were about to get a whole lot worse.

Spain, June 1976 and The Netherlands, August 2022

The summer of 1976 was one of the hottest on record in Europe. Nevertheless, Mum had booked a holiday to Spain to celebrate my tenth birthday. This was to be my first experience of being abroad.

As I walked on the sand, the soles of my feet began to sizzle. Never before had I experienced such intense heat. Desperate to find something cool – and quickly – the voice in my head screamed, The Sea!

Gulp! A steep incline from the beach to the sea had taken me by surprise. With the seabed beyond reach, I was completely out of my depth. In a state of deep panic, I began flapping my arms around, attempting to stay afloat.

But without my armbands, I couldn't swim. My cries for help dulled as I swallowed mouthful after mouthful of salt water.

Mum, who was swimming with friends just a few metres away, quickly realised what was happening and screamed for help.

Within minutes I was lying on the beach surrounded by worried onlookers. Vaguely recalling the scramble to pull me out of the water, I was slowly but surely resuming a normal breathing rhythm while spitting out any remaining seawater. Every ounce of energy had been sapped out of me. I was exhausted.

Fast forward to the summer of 2022.

Having dared to return to the water after the Spain incident, I was now able to swim unaided, but my technique was awkward. Spurred on by the cancer diagnosis, I decided it was time to learn to swim properly. My neighbour Maureen became my swimming mate.

Buying swimming goggles was the easy part. The ticket and locker systems, both in Dutch, less so. Maureen to the rescue! Then came the hardest part. Placing my head under water without inhaling and swallowing a mouthful of chlorinated water was no easy task. For several weeks, choking and spluttering became the norm, but then came a breakthrough. I began to swim like a fish, doing five continuous strokes under water. Progress – albeit still not using the right technique.

"Wij kunnen dit." (We can do this.) The encouragement Maureen and I gave each other en route to the swimming baths was priceless. Within a few months we were both swimming like pros, with our heads under the water, one stroke to one breath. We were proud of ourselves.

Sink or swim?

In Spain, I sank, but years later, thanks to Maureen, I not only mastered the Dutch ticket and locker systems, but I was also swimming like a pro.

Sink or swim? I say a categorical "No, no way and no thank you!" How about you?

I'm sure, like me, you recognise this well-known idiom. However, sink *or* swim is not the only choice you have when dealing with change. There's an alternative – sink *then* swim. Know that when managing change while living abroad, first you sink and then you swim.

You Are No Stranger to Change

According to Heraclitus, "The only constant in life is change." Nothing in life stays the same. Change is indeed an integral and unavoidable part of life.

You have been coping with change from the moment you were born. Let's stop and think about that for a minute. You arrived in the world after months of confidently swimming in the warm waters of your mother's belly. When you left those waters, the first few weeks involved you being passed from person to person. All you saw was face upon face glaring down at you. All you heard was "So cute" or "He looks just like you" or "She has a lot of hair". Some of those faces would get *way* too close for comfort, and some of those voices would be *way* too loud. It was all a bit scary, and it's likely all you wanted was to return to the warm waters of your mother's belly. But there was no going back. The journey of change in your life continued.

At various times in your life, perhaps …

- There was a new addition to your family – a brother, a sister, twins or more.
- A family member died.
- You separated or divorced.
- You or a relative became seriously ill.
- You needed to find a job.

And perhaps at one time in your life, you not only moved home, you moved home *and* country. Without doubt, you have experienced wave upon wave of change in your life – in your world *and* in our wider world.

Our wider world is the world where we co-exist with billions of others. It's the world in which we have little influence and control – the world we don't and can't possibly fully understand. Changes in our wider world are mostly unforeseeable, and how we subsequently deal with these is far from easy.

Within our wider world exists *your* world. In this world, you co-exist with a few others, some of whom remain with you for a long time, while others come and go. They are your family, friends, acquaintances, neighbours and work and study colleagues. This world you understand better than our wider world. What's more, you have influence within it and, to some extent, a degree of control. Changes in your world may be foreseeable, but like our wider world, these are far from easy to deal with.

You are no stranger to change – in both our wider world and your world.

Change in Our Wider World

We live in a Volatile, Uncertain, Complex and Ambiguous world – a VUCA world. This acronym, created by the US Army War College, is based on the management theories of Warren Bennis and Burt Nanus, professors in business management. At the time of writing, it describes perfectly Our Wider World. We are in a constant flux of change from which there would seem to be no escape.

Profound changes in Our Wider World that have impacted our lives in recent times include:

2019 – The Covid-19 Pandemic.
2020 – Brexit. The UK left the European Union (EU).
2021 – Rise in Global Inflation.
2022 – The Russian-Ukrainian War.
2022 – Global Energy Crisis.
2023 – Israel and Palestine (Hamas) War.
2023 – USA and Iran Proxy War: The Red Sea Crisis.
2023 – Extreme elemental incidents, including fire, flooding and storm-force winds.
2024 – Unrest around the world, including farmers' protests, transport and health service strikes and a lack of trust in governments and international organisations.

Brexit (Britain's exit from the EU) came about following the 2016 referendum when UK citizens were invited to vote on whether the UK should remain in or exit the EU. In January 2020, after a three-and-a-half-year transition period, the UK exited the EU. Here's how Brexit impacted my life:

Brexit – The Netherlands

The fallout I experienced from the Brexit referendum reminds me of the James Bond movie No Time to Die – when Bond was locked in a cabin on a boat blown up by villains. As always, Bond survived.

At the mercy of the ocean and sinking into the abyss, feelings of anger, sadness and loneliness got the better of me. I felt abandoned by the UK, my country of birth. Brexit had engulfed me and was impacting my identity and my sense of belonging. The threat of being deported, being separated from my husband and being stripped of my EU citizenship was real.

But then, as I resurfaced from the abyss, hope began to seep through me.

Being married to a Dutchman and having successfully completed the Dutch integration exams became my lifesaver. I could apply for Dutch citizenship. Without hesitation I submitted the application along with the extortionate just-short-of nine hundred euro fee. In January 2021 I became a Dutch citizen and my EU citizenship was reinstated. I once again felt calm.

Speaking with other British citizens living abroad, I learned that Brexit had had a similar impact on their lives. They too had been angry and sad. They too had felt lonely. We'd all been in the same boat, that boat blown up by villains.

Sink or swim? First we sank and then we swam.

> "To alleviate any fears of being kicked out of Spain, my wife and I applied for and got Spanish residency."
>
> **Simon in Spain**

> "I definitely felt a sense of shock and of irreparable loss. It really did feel like I was grieving."
>
> **Kate in France**

At the end of the Brexit transition period, a tsunami hit every corner of the world. That tsunami was the Covid-19 Pandemic. Here's how the Pandemic impacted my life:

> ### The Covid-19 Pandemic – The Netherlands
>
> *The Pandemic, like for so many others around the world, prevented me from seeing family members for years.*
>
> *On January 2nd 2020, I waved goodbye to Mum at Schiphol airport, believing we would see one another again in just over two months. I could not have been more wrong, and the months that followed were excruciatingly painful.*
>
> *As an only child with a mum who lived alone, the feeling of helplessness consumed me. Unlike Brexit, there was nothing I could do. With travel restrictions that changed at what seemed like daily intervals, the situation was both confusing and distressing. I was being prevented from leaving the Netherlands and from entering the UK, and Mum wasn't permitted to leave the UK or enter the Netherlands.*
>
> *Video calls were great but were no substitute for face-to-face contact. Keeping our hopes alive was crucial. "We're one day closer to seeing one another," I said every time Mum and I spoke.*
>
> *In February 2022, some 774 days after saying our goodbyes, Mum and I were finally reunited.*
>
> *Sink or swim? First we sank and then we swam.*

Both Brexit and the Covid-19 Pandemic threw Volatility, Uncertainty, Complexity and Ambiguity my way:

- I faced wave upon wave of change. These were far from calm, constant and stable times. They were Volatile.

- The waters were uncharted. There was no plan, no map and no known route. There was only Uncertainty.
- There were undercurrents. These circumstances were not simple, straightforward or obvious to navigate. They were Complex.
- Thick fog rolled over the waves of change. These situations were unclear, not obvious or self-explanatory. They were Ambiguous.

VUCA is by far the best acronym to describe change in Our Wider World. It's also a highly appropriate acronym to describe change that occurs in *your* world.

Change in Your World

Change not only occurs in Our Wider World but also in Your World.

Changes falling into the category of *life's most stressful situations*, namely, *moving home, the death of a relative, divorce and separation, ill-health* and *finding a job*, have seen me and others I know sink to the depths of the ocean. Laying on that ocean floor, believing there was no way back to the surface, I have felt anxious, vulnerable and pessimistic. These changes included:

1969 – My father left Mum and me to be with another woman. I was just three years old.
1973 – Mum re-married and we moved to another city where I started a new school.
1975 – Great-grandmother was killed in a hit-and-run accident.
1977 – First grandparent died.
1979 – Moved home for the sixth time to live with my third father figure. I was thirteen years old.
2003 – Hans, my Dutch husband, was diagnosed with cancer.
2008 – Had a five-kilo benign ovarian cyst and ovary removed.
2011 – When our second IVF treatment failed, Hans and I realised we couldn't have children.
2013 – Repatriated to work in the UK without Hans.
2016 – Diagnosed with breast cancer. An operation and radiotherapy followed.
2016 – Stopped working due to ill-health.
2016 – Biological father died.

2019 – Stepfather died.
2021 – Moved home for the twenty-fourth time in my life.
2022 – Diagnosed with breast cancer for the second time and stopped working as a result.
2022 – Uncle died suddenly.
2022 – Anette, my breast cancer buddy, died.
2022 & 2024 – Hans diagnosed with curable skin cancer.

Conversely, some of the changes in my life have seen me swimming confidently. Surfing the waves of change, I have been excited, confident and optimistic. These changes have included:

1989 – Relocated to the USA, becoming an expatriate for the first time.
2002 – Met Hans on a singles holiday in Tanzania. At that time, Hans, originally from the Netherlands, was living in Norway.
2003 – Sold my home, left my job, started my own business and moved to Norway to be with Hans.
2004 – Got married. Hurrah!
2013 – Successful completion of master's degree in International HR (Human Resources) and Globalisation.
2014 – Secured my first HR job in Norway.
2016 – Relocated to the Netherlands.
2018 – Hooch, a Hungarian Vizsla, our first dog, joined the Schoormans family.
2018 – Started my own business for the second time.
2021 – Obtained Dutch nationality.

Change has regularly impacted My World. How about you?

 **SWIMMING LESSON ONE**
Major Changes in Your Life

In this, your first Swimming Lesson, you are asked to recall the major changes you have experienced in your life.

List below the major changes that have occurred in both the Wider World and in Your World – before and after relocating abroad. Include changes in all aspects of your life: your family, your work and education, your health and your hobbies.

Why Change Is Difficult

Even though change repeatedly impacts your life, dealing with it is far from easy. But why? In her book *How To Do The Work*, a book focused on navigating adverse behaviours brought about by unfavourable situations in life, Dr Nicole LePera argues, "We are not evolutionarily wired for change."

As an HR professional, I have on many occasions been at the forefront of implementing organisational change programmes, programmes leading to job losses. Sheepishly, I confess I tended to focus on the *process* of change. Why wouldn't I? Adhering to policy and process to avoid legal claims was the number one concern. But reflecting on the times when I shared news of job losses, I recall the fear, anxiety and dismay on the faces of the employees.

Failing to recognise and take into consideration emotional reactions to change is harsh, inconsiderate and unjustifiable. We need only remind ourselves of the Covid-19 Pandemic to fully appreciate this. With imposed lockdowns, the wearing of facemasks, and vaccinations, a deluge of palpable emotions came to the surface. Change is much more than adhering to policy and process. Change is, unquestionably, about managing emotions.

Thoughts and Emotions

Changes in life range from minor incidents to total transformations of normality.

Resisting change is natural. Unnerved and unsettled, you view the change as disruptive and dramatic. Your reactions may include:

- "This can't be. It's not right and it's not fair."
- "Shit! You've got to be kidding."
- "No way! I don't want anything to do with this."

You are desperate to cling on to normality, to retain stability, and an influx of negative Thoughts and Emotions take hold. Your behaviour, motivation and will to do things all falter. You are sinking.

Yes, change dissolves the familiar, but if you view it through a different lens, it can be stimulating, innovative and exciting. Then your reactions may include:

- "Bring it on."
- "This is exactly what I need right now."
- "This is *sooooo* exciting. Let's get to it."

Possibilities and opportunities wash over any Thoughts of clinging on to the familiar. An influx of positive Thoughts and Emotions ignite within you. Your behaviour, motivation and will to do things all blossom. Energised, you swim through the change with ease.

This dichotomy illustrates how the way you perceive change influences your Thoughts and Emotions in different ways. Let's dive deeper to learn more.

What Are Thoughts?

Thoughts are "the internal representation of events" says Charles Egerton Osgood, an American social psychologist, in Nicky Hayes and Sue Orrell's book *Psychology*. Comprising ideas, views, opinions and beliefs, our Thoughts are in a constant state of ebb and flow. Playing out worst-case and what-if scenarios and often coupled with self-talk, we have thousands of Thoughts every day.

Upon waking one Saturday morning, the following Thoughts raced through my mind.

It's Saturday, my day off. Saturday's pizza day but we have no onions to make the sauce. Supermarket, then a trip to the beach with Hans and Hooch ... our happy place. A good walk and maybe a swim is just what I need. I'm getting excited just thinking about that. Yes, but you have a presentation to deliver next week and you haven't even started preparing for it. You know how important this is. It's Mum's eightieth birthday next year. I wonder what she wants to do? I'll call her later. Back to that presentation. I feel sick just thinking about the amount of work it requires. I enjoy delivering presentations but preparing is another matter. You haven't got time to go to the beach. I know, but it'll be good for me. Yes, but ...

As fast as a Thought arises, it weakens and disappears, yet when you give it attention, by interpreting, judging or analysing it or by replaying the situation over and over in your mind, you make it stronger. And that's when your emotions come to the surface.

What Are Emotions?

Books, articles or an internet search on the subject of Emotions will bring you face-to-face with a long list, which may include the following:

Agitation	Eagerness	Indignation	Ruthlessness
Anxiety	Envy	Irritation	Satisfaction
Bliss	Gratitude	Kindness	Shame
Calm	Greed	Nostalgia	Shock
Depression	Hope	Offence	Surprise
Desire	Humility	Relaxation	Tolerance

Eckhart Tolle, author of *The Power of Now*, states that "an emotion usually represents an amplified and energised thought pattern", one that "wants to take over you, and it usually succeeds". For example, when a Thought alerts you to a change in your surroundings or in yourself and you view it as a threat, your nervous system goes into a state of high alert. You experience a fight-freeze-flight response, meaning you will do one of three things: face the situation head-on, stop and do nothing, or run away.

Several theorists have looked at the connection between Thoughts and Emotions. James-Lange, Cannon-Bard, Schachter-Singer, and Lazarus all agree that a stimulus must happen before a physiological reaction (a physical or nervous reaction or sensation in the body such as your heart beating faster, nausea, muscles tensing, increased alertness) and an emotional reaction occur. The order in which the physiological or emotional reaction occurs – one before the other, simultaneously, or after you assess what is happening – differs from one theory to the next. Thankfully, we can have some Thoughts that invoke no physiological or emotional reaction. If that were not the case, we would experience the same number of Emotions as Thoughts and perhaps experience multiple Emotions simultaneously. And that, quite frankly, would be exhausting.

Now, back to my Saturday morning Thoughts. The ones resulting in a physical or nervous reaction were:

- Going to the beach – I was *excited*.
- Preparing for the presentation – I felt *sick*.

And while I am unable to recall my emotional state at the time, I suspect that:

- Going to the beach – My excitement brought with it *contentment* and *happiness*.
- Preparing for the presentation – My nausea brought with it *anxiety*.

Like Thoughts, Emotions increase in intensity when you give them attention. Replaying the situation again and again in your mind allows Emotions to stew and fester. Subsequently, when they are negative, pessimistic and gloomy, they impede your behaviour and, therefore, your ability to deal with change effectively.

Get Leggy with Your Thoughts and Emotions

While you may not be able to control what is happening to you, you do have the ability to control how you respond. In 2012, under the instruction of renowned coach Richard Bandler, I became a Neuro-Linguistic Programming (NLP) master practitioner, learning how to switch Thoughts and Emotions in an instant. Making a conscious effort to switch your negative, pessimistic and gloomy Thoughts and Emotions to positive, optimistic and motivating ones enables you to break the pattern of viewing change as disruptive, chaotic and dramatic. Viewing it instead as stimulating, innovative and exciting, you are better equipped to manage the change. This I call Getting Leggy.

Getting Leggy I liken to the vertical position in synchronised swimming, when your body is upside down in the water and only your legs are visible above the surface. By turning your negative Thoughts and Emotions upside down, you make them positive.

So, let's Get Leggy.

First, read the following steps to the end and then follow each step one by one. For better results, record the instructions, then listen to and follow the instructions with your eyes closed.

1. Stop what you are doing. Acknowledge the negative Thought or Emotion. With a smile, say out loud, "I am aware of *sadness*," or whatever negative Thought or Emotion you are experiencing.

2. Visualise a large red STOP sign. Now focus on your breath. Take a deep belly breath in and out, envisaging the Thought or Emotion dissolving as you breathe out. Repeat three times. Your negative Thought or Emotion has melted away. Now hum a few notes.

3. Visualise a large green GO sign. Visualise a positive Thought or Emotion and smile. Take a deep belly breath in, envisaging absorbing that Thought or Emotion. Breathe out.

4. Say out loud, or better still, sing out loud, "I am aware of *happiness*," or whatever positive Thought or Emotion has surfaced. Repeat three times.

5. Visualise yourself embracing the positive Thought or Emotion.

Here are some examples of how negative Thoughts and Emotions can be turned into positive ones.

From fear to confidence
Fear is a natural reaction to change. You don't always understand what is happening, why it is happening and how it will affect you. The word FEAR, an acronym for False Evidence Appearing Real, can bring about dark and debilitating Thoughts and Emotions. Conversely, FEAR is also an acronym for Face Everything And Rise, instilling confidence within. When you are curious, wanting to know more about what you're experiencing, positive Thoughts and Emotions surface.

When I plunged into the sea in Spain in 1976, panic engulfed me. Splashing around in emotional waves, unable to swim, was both scary and exhausting. Years later, I was swimming like a pro. *Get Leggy with fear and become confident.*

From anger to calm
Anger is another natural reaction to change. You scream and shout:

- "Why is this happening to me?"
- "Why now?"

Conversely, you could calmly ask yourself:

- "Why not me?"
- "Why not now?"

Once the shock of the second cancer diagnosis subsided, I became angry. I was angry with myself for not having raised the alarm earlier, having instinctively known for months that something wasn't right. However, my anger wasn't going to change anything. It was time to view the situation as an opportunity to make profound and sustainable changes in my life. It was time to overhaul my health and well-being, to bring calmness into my life. *Get Leggy with anger and become calm.*

From confusion to clarity
Confusion is another natural reaction to change. When you are not able to see the whole picture, when you don't appreciate what's happening and don't have all the facts, confusion takes hold. Conversely, when you ask questions and look at the bigger picture, you begin to understand what's happening and why. You gain clarity.

In 2008 I was informed I had a cyst on my ovary. Both the cyst *and* the ovary needed to be removed, but I didn't understand why. Confused, I questioned the doctor. The five-kilo cyst had damaged the ovary. It was absolutely necessary to remove them both. *Get Leggy with confusion to gain clarity.*

From loneliness to connections
Loneliness is often a consequence of change. Your family and friends may never have lived abroad. You convince yourself they don't understand your new life and what you're experiencing. As you distance yourself, cease contact even, loneliness sets in. Conversely, connecting with friends, family and others to seek support and to ask for help enables loneliness to subside.

Remember my Brexit experience when I felt I was coping with my identity and sense of belonging crisis alone? After speaking with other British citizens living abroad, it became clear they felt the same. Connections are priceless. *Get Leggy with loneliness and benefit from connections.*

From sadness to happiness

Sadness is yet another consequence of change. Change brings endings and a feeling of loss as familiarity fades away or abruptly ends. Conversely, change brings possibilities and opportunities to embrace the unknown and the unfamiliar – to be happy.

From a young age, I have experienced the passing of family members. While I've shed many a tear, I have also smiled and sometimes laughed, recalling happy times. Let sadness dissolve and happiness shine through. *Get Leggy with sadness and embrace happiness.*

🏊 SWIMMING LESSON TWO
Change and Your Emotions

Having identified the major changes in your life in Swimming Lesson One, Swimming Lesson Two focuses on the Emotions that surface when change occurs in your life.

List below the Emotions you recall when you reflect on the major changes that have impacted your life. To help you get started, when I received news that my grandma had died, the Emotions that surfaced included:

Frustration

Anger

Relief

Calm

Be Confident, Be Calm, Gain Clarity, Benefit from Connections and Embrace Happiness

Change is an inevitability in life and is laden with Volatility, Uncertainty, Complexity and Ambiguity. Few would deny how difficult change can be. However, you – and many others before you – have not only survived change but thrived as a consequence.

You *have* the ability to deal with change in your life, to deal with everything that is thrown at you. Furthermore, Getting Leggy with those pesky, debilitating negative, pessimistic and gloomy Thoughts and Emotions means you are better equipped to deal with change. Knowing this, you feel confident and calm, gain clarity, benefit from connections, *and* feel happy when dealing with life's most stressful situations while living abroad.

Chapter Summary

In this chapter you learned ...

- To calm the choppy, emotional waves within when change impacts your life.
- You are no stranger to change.
- Change is unavoidable and inevitable both in Our Wider World and in Your World.
- Change is laden with Volatility, Uncertainty, Complexity and Ambiguity.
- To Get Leggy because change is more about managing Emotions than adhering to policy and process. Turning your negative, pessimistic and gloomy Thoughts and Emotions into positive, optimistic and motivating ones reframes your approach to change.
- When profound change impacts your life, it's not about choosing between sink or swim but instead knowing that first you sink and then you swim.

In this chapter you have completed two Swimming Lessons.

Congratulate yourself. You've earned your first swimming medal.

Useful Resources

- Listen to *Fear Is a Liar.* Zach Williams. https://www.youtube.com/watch?v=1srs1YoTVzs
- Listen to *Theories of Emotion.* Collin Testing and Psychological Services. https://www.youtube.com/watch?v=qDYz32srgsU
- Read *Change Management: A Critical Perspective. Chapter Ten,* Resistance to Change. Mark Hughes. 2010. Chartered Institute of Personnel and Development.
- Read *Embracing Change: How to Build Resilience and Make Change Work for You.* Dr. Harry Barry. 2021. Orion Spring.
- Read *Feel the Fear and Do It Anyway.* Susan Jeffers. 2012. Penguin Random House.
- Read *Guide to Trance-Formation: Make Your Life Great. Chapter One,* Patterns, Learning and Change and *Chapter Two,* Doing More of What Works. Richard Bandler. 2008. Harper Collins Publishers Ltd.
- Read *How to Change Absolutely Anything: Practical Techniques to Make Real and Lasting Changes.* Damian Hughes. 2013. Skyhorse Publishing.
- Read *The Liquid Thinking Survival Guide to Change.* Damian Hughes. 2013. Skyhorse Publishing.
- Read *The Little Book of Calm.* Paul Wilson. 2014. Octopus Publishing Group Ltd.
- Read *The Little Book of Psychology.* Emily Ralls and Caroline Riggs. 2019. Summersdale Publishers Ltd.
- Read more about VUCA here: https://usawc.libanswers.com/faq/84869
- Watch *A Hand Model of the Brain.* Dr Daniel Siegel. www.youtube.com/watch?v=gm9CIJ74Oxw

A Ripple of Laughter

What did one ocean say to another?
Nothing. It simply waved.

Source: https://www.goodbadjokes.com/jokes/what-did-one-ocean-say-to-the-other-ocean

CHAPTER TWO
Navigating Culture

"A nation's culture resides in the hearts and in the soul of its people."
Mahatma Gandhi
Indian lawyer famous for his non-violence philosophy and achieving political and economic freedom from Britain

The Globalisation Conundrum

We live in a global world.

When you relocated abroad for the first time, you will likely have given little to no thought to the differences between your home and your host country. I know I didn't.

USA, September 1989 to September 1990

After graduating in 1989, I emigrated to the USA. Working for Marriott Hotels in the beautiful state of Rhode Island, the original location of the America's Cup sailing race, was my first living abroad experience.

I knew little about the USA, but nothing was going to get in the way of what I considered to be a once in a lifetime opportunity. The prospect of working in the USA for a year was both scary and exciting.

Despite a common language, there were some slight and often embarrassing differences between British and American English. Pants were trousers, rubbers were condoms, and being pissed meant you were angry – not drunk.

Despite a desire to explore the USA, life was all about work. Working long hours and accruing a total of just ten days' annual leave was the norm. I could take time off or receive holiday pay. I chose the latter. Time off could wait until the end of my work year.

Despite a shared language, the style of communication was different. Americans communicated directly, getting to the point quickly, and there was less formality. First names were used at work, unlike in the UK, where Mr and Mrs were standard practice.

I also learned:

- *I had to pay to open a bank account.*
- *To write dates with the month first.*
- *Calling home was expensive (the internet was in its infancy).*
- *I could shop out-of-hours in 7-Eleven stores.*
- *Leaving a tip was almost obligatory.*

Living in the USA was different from living in my home country, the UK.

Norway, April 2003 to July 2016

In April 2003, after having sold my home and resigned from my job, I relocated to Norway to live with Hans. This was my second living abroad experience, and this time I had no plans to return to the UK. The prospect of living in Norway with my new partner was both scary and exciting.

Despite having passed my advanced driving test, I needed to get used to driving on the opposite side of the road. While the thought of doing so was daunting, I simply got in the car and drove. To my surprise and delight there was no tailgating and there were no racing drivers. Driving at a safe distance and at a comfortable speed was indicative of a society valuing space and not wanting to be rushed.

> *Despite doing my utmost to be polite and friendly, I discovered that Norwegians are private people. Making eye contact and engaging in conversation with my neighbour when we were on the bus together was pointless. Sitting alone, it was clear she didn't want to be disturbed.*
>
> *Even though I was working for an international company, the Norwegian work culture was different from what I was used to:*
>
> - *Smart casual, as opposed to formal business dress, was the norm.*
> - *Leaving work at 4pm on Friday to go skiing or hiking in the mountains with family, as opposed to 6pm or later to go to the pub with work colleagues, was standard practice.*
> - *Socialising with work colleagues was reserved for teambuilding events and the Christmas party, called Julebord.*
>
> *Living in Norway was different from living in my home country, the UK.*

We live in a global world, don't we?

Trading blocs like the European Union and the Association of Southeastern Asian Nations (ASEAN), rapid technological advancement and multinational corporations have all crossed national borders and are steering the way towards convergence, homogeneity and similarity within Our Wider World. Globalisation is dissolving and lessening the differences between countries.

But wait, what about culture and language? Globalisation is not dissolving or lessening these. They are unconquerable barriers to globalisation that can't be extinguished. Remember how each country implemented their own travel restrictions during the Covid-19 Pandemic? Divergence, heterogeneity and dissimilarity exist within Our Wider World.

Yes, we live in a global world, but within Our World, both sameness *and* difference exist. Forgive yourself, therefore, for believing there would be little to no difference between your home and your host country when you relocated abroad. Culture and language are the overarching reasons for the differences.

Above and Below the Surface of the Water

So, what is culture exactly?

In her book *Managing Across Cultures*, CM Solomon defines culture as "the way people act, what they think" and "what they believe". While culture is visible in what we do and how we do it, what we think and believe remain invisible.

Culture is a complex concept. However, by examining it from above *and* below the water's surface, its complexities can be unravelled.

Located above the surface of the water are the explicit and visible aspects of a country's culture – the climate, food and language, to name but a few. The climate: maybe it rains a lot, it's hot, it's windy. The food: maybe it's bland, it's spicy, it's greasy. The language: maybe some words are familiar, while others are not. These cultural aspects are relatively easy to relate to and to understand. They are the reason why we believe similarity exists in Our Wider World and why we believe life abroad is not so different from life back home.

Located below the surface of the water are the implicit and invisible aspects of a country's culture – the beliefs and values of a country's natives. These aspects are often underestimated and misunderstood. Remember my Norwegian neighbour sitting alone on the bus, minding her own business? She was valuing her space and privacy. I, on the other hand, viewed her behaviour as unfriendly. I was viewing her behaviour from my own cultural perspective, a natural thing to do when you live abroad.

The implicit and invisible aspects of a country's culture are often difficult to relate to and to comprehend – or so we are led to believe …

These aspects manifest in behaviours and communication styles. When you observe and copy these, you embark on a journey of understanding your host country's culture. After many years of living in Norway, I too found myself sitting alone on the bus, minding my own business. I was valuing my own space and privacy. I was adapting to my host country's culture.

🏊 SWIMMING LESSON THREE
Cultural Similarities and Differences

In Swimming Lesson Three you are asked to compare the cultures of your home and your host country. What's similar and what's different?

In the space below, list the visible and invisible similarities and differences between your home and your host country.

Similarities	Differences
For example: English is spoken in both my home and my host country.	*For example:* In my home country, the UK, I chatted with my neighbour and strangers on the bus. In Norway I remained silent.

Similarities	Differences

Life abroad *is* different. You see, feel, hear, taste, smell and sense difference. Without question, the explicit and implicit, and the visible and invisible aspects of your host country's culture impact your life abroad. In 2010, after training to become an intercultural trainer and starting a master's degree in International HR and Globalisation, I began to appreciate why I had found the USA easier to adjust to than Norway. It was all about the cultural aspects. The USA was culturally and linguistically more like the UK than Norway.

Navigating culture requires an understanding and appreciation of both the similarities and the differences between the cultures of your home and your host country.

Cultural Waves

The profound impact of moving home (one of life's most stressful situations) *and* moving country is often underestimated. This journey of change, commonly referred to as the 'integration journey', comprises several stages of shock – *culture shock*. Not always sequential or separated from each other, I refer to these stages as Cultural Waves.

As you disengage from your home country's culture and begin to engage with an unfamiliar host country culture, strong, frothy emotional waves ferment within you, and sometimes these waves have sharp teeth. Each Cultural Wave creates an imbalance in your life. You may, at best, feel like you are pushing water uphill and, at worst, like you are being swept away by a tidal wave. Remember to turn the negative, pessimistic and gloomy Thoughts and Emotions that surface into positive, optimistic and motivating ones by Getting Leggy (see *Chapter One*). You will then move forwards on your integration journey, swimming confidently with these Cultural Waves.

Dipping Your Toes in the Water

Relocating abroad ignites feelings of excitement and apprehension. Venturing into the unknown, exploring the ins and outs of your host country through rose-coloured glasses, you disregard any differences between your home and host country. *Dipping your toes in the water*, you are checking to see if this new chapter in your life is real. Get Leggy with any negative, pessimistic and gloomy Thoughts and Emotions you encounter.

A Fish Out of Water

The simple things in life like shopping, going to the doctors and catching a train have become enormous undertakings. Things in your host country are not the same as they were back home. The way things are done is different. You know only one way – the way things were done in your home country – but this way no longer works. As your sense of reality and familiarity fade away, your self-belief and self-confidence plummet. Like *a fish out of water*, you feel vulnerable, disorientated and overwhelmed. Get Leggy with any negative, pessimistic and gloomy Thoughts and Emotions you encounter.

Treading Water

Having established new routines and a new rhythm in your life, you've found that the simple things have, once again, become manageable. However, you haven't, as yet, mastered everything. Frustrations, regrets and resentment creep in as you realise undercurrents of difference remain. You begin to question why you relocated abroad. You want to go home, but you *are* home, aren't you? Calm and happy one minute, angry and sad the next, your Thoughts and Emotions continue to bob up and down on the waves of change. *Treading water*, you remain unsure whether to head north, south, east or west. Get Leggy with any negative, pessimistic and gloomy Thoughts and Emotions you encounter.

Swimming Against the Tide

The behaviour of a local has offended you, embarrassed you, shamed you even. Shaken and knocked sideways, you are in shock. The incident, directly clashing with your own beliefs and values, brings about feelings of inadequacy, discomfort and self-consciousness. You become hostile towards the locals and possibly even towards your family and friends. *Swimming against the tide* between your home and host country cultures, you are exhausted. You retreat into your shell, isolating yourself from Our Wider World. Get Leggy with any negative, pessimistic and gloomy Thoughts and Emotions you encounter.

Surfing the Waves of Change

Having taken a deep dive to understand the whys of your host country (why the locals do what they do), you now fully appreciate the scale of the differences between your host and home countries. Cracking open your protective shell, you attentively observe and copy the locals' behaviours and take note of their communication style. What was once strange is now familiar. *Surfing the waves of change*, you are adapting to and embracing your host country's culture. Get Leggy with any negative, pessimistic and gloomy Thoughts and Emotions you encounter.

🏊 SWIMMING LESSON FOUR
From One Cultural Wave to Another

In Swimming Lesson Four you are asked to identify where you are right now on your integration journey and to Get Leggy with any negative Thoughts and Emotions you are experiencing.

Circle below the Cultural Wave(s) you are currently experiencing on your integration journey. Perhaps you are bobbing back and forth between two or more Cultural Waves?

Dipping Your Toes in the Water

A Fish Out of Water

Treading Water

Swimming Against the Tide

Surfing the Waves of Change

List any negative Thoughts and Emotions you are currently experiencing and Get Leggy with these.

Thought(s) and Emotion(s)	Get Leggy
For example:	*For example:*
Treading Water – I get frustrated and angry when I can't find the right word or when I make a mistake when speaking Dutch. I tell myself: I must do better.	I say to myself: The locals understand me even when I make mistakes. I'm doing my best and that's good enough.

Thought(s) and Emotion(s)	Get Leggy

Chapter Summary

In this chapter you learned ...

- How to navigate culture.
- Globalisation is not a tidal wave that has created sameness in the world. Sameness and difference co-exist.
- Culture is a complex phenomenon that creates difference in the world.
- Culture comprises explicit/implicit and visible/invisible aspects.
- The implicit and invisible aspects of culture become explicit and visible through behaviours and communication styles.
- To adapt to your host country's culture by copying the behaviours and communication styles of locals.
- How to navigate through the differences between the cultures of your home and host country.
- How to swim with Cultural Waves – the stages of shock on the integration journey.
- What culture shock is.

In this chapter you have completed two Swimming Lessons.

Congratulate yourself. You've earned your second swimming medal.

Useful Resources

- Read *Basic Concepts of Intercultural Communication. Chapter One*, Intercultural Communication: A Current Perspective. Milton Bennett. 1989. Intercultural Press Inc.
- Read *Kiss, Bow, or Shake Hands*. Terri Morrison and Wayne A Conaway. 2006. Adams Media.
- Read *The Art of Crossing Cultures*. Page 85, A Model of Cross-Cultural Interaction, *Chapter One*, Country Shock, *Chapter Two*, Culture Shock and *Chapter Five*, The Problem Solved. Craig Storti. 2001. Intercultural Press Inc.
- Read *The Art of Coming Home*. Craig Storti. 2003. Intercultural Press Inc. (For repatriation.)

- Read *The 7 Mental Images of National Culture. Chapter Two*, Hofstede's 6D Model of National Culture. Huib Wursten. 2019. Hofstede Insights.
- Watch *Culture Shock and The Cultural Adaptation Cycle.* The Global Society. https://www.youtube.com/watch?v=g-ef-xhC_bU
- Watch *How Culture Drives Behaviours.* Julien S. Bourrelle. https://www.youtube.com/watch?v=l-Yy6poJ2zs

A Ripple of Laughter

What's the best thing about Switzerland?
The flag. It's a big plus.

Source: https://punstoppable.com/Switzerland-puns

PART TWO

DIVE DEEP INTO WHO YOU REALLY ARE

> "Be yourself; everyone else is already taken."

Oscar Wilde
Irish writer, playwright and poet

CHAPTER THREE

Crystal Clear Waters: Your Values

"Open your arms to change but don't let go of your values."
Dalai Lama XIV
Leader of Tibetan Buddhism representing peace and compassion

What Are Values?

Values are:

- Your life principles.
- What define you.
- Your standards of behaviour.
- What motivate you.
- A part of your identity.

According to Elvis Presley, an American singer and actor, "Values are like fingerprints. Nobody's are the same, but you leave them all over everything you do." Your values are unique to you and they steer your behaviours. Pointing you in the direction of your preferences, they are solid and reliable indicators of what is important to you and what you believe to be right. Or to put it another way, Values steer you away from what isn't important to you and what you believe to be wrong.

Health, happiness, love, and physical and economic security are the most important Values in life according to Dov Elizur and Abraham Sagie in their article 'Facets of Personal Values: A Structural Analysis of Life and Work Values'. If you look at these closely, you'll notice they are innate Values directly aligned to basic needs. You strive to be healthy, to be happy, to be loved and to love, and to feel secure in life.

Books, articles or an internet search on the subject of Values will bring you face-to-face with list upon list of Values, which may include the following:

Accountability	Diversity	Independence	Reliability
Adaptability	Fairness	Integrity	Respect
Compassion	Friendship	Learning	Responsibility
Competence	Fun	Love	Service
Confidence	Growth	Patience	Spirituality
Creativity	Health	Perseverance	Truth
Courage	Honesty	Purpose	Uniqueness
Curiosity	Humility	Quality	Wisdom

From Where Do Values Originate?

Values originate from several sources.

Values describe cultural groups, societies and individuals. Your Values originate not only from your family and your home country's culture but also from your teachers, friends, work colleagues and your host country's culture.

Values also originate from your beliefs. Mahatma Gandhi's famous quote, "Your beliefs become your thoughts, your thoughts become your words, your words become your actions, your actions become your habits, your habits become your Values, your Values become your destiny," clearly expresses how beliefs manifest as Values. When a belief is of significance, when you believe it to be true and when your attachment to that belief grows over time, it is likely to be one of your Values. For example, if you strongly believe in keeping healthy, you commit to eating and drinking produce that is good for you, you exercise regularly and you may also meditate and practise mindfulness. Through your actions, keeping healthy, a deep-rooted belief, becomes one of your Values. But not all your beliefs become Values. You may, for example, believe that to be healthy you need to embrace healthy eating, exercise regularly, meditate and practise mindfulness, yet *you fail to take action*. Through your inaction, keeping healthy remains a belief. It does not become one of your Values.

Values sometimes originate from a lack of something in your life. When there is a void in your life, something you crave and are motivated to fulfil, you take action to embrace the missing something. For example, each of the Living Abroad Stories in *Chapter Five* shares a common void: connections. Almost everyone stressed the importance of connecting with others.

Values Fluctuate

Some people argue that Values remain stable throughout your life, while others argue they change. I suggest both are true.

Here's an example of how *independence* has remained a constant value throughout my life.

> As an only child and a child who lived without a father figure for several years, I have learned to be self-sufficient. My mum taught me several life skills, from wiring plugs to painting and decorating, skills instilling a robust inner belief of *I can do this and I can do this alone*. I love to be the captain of my own ship, to have the freedom to do things my way. Becoming an expat for the first time in 1989, flying across the Atlantic Ocean to the USA with little knowledge of what lay ahead, plus twice running my own business, are examples of how the value of *independence* has been a constant in my life.

And here's an example of how *rest* has become of paramount importance to me in recent months – but hasn't always been so.

> As a child, I loved being in the garden with my grandparents, and I like to think I was of some help – despite sometimes pulling the heads off their neighbours' flowers. Later in life, when I became a workaholic, gardening was less important – that was, until the second cancer diagnosis. Since then, tending to flowers and shrubs, growing my own vegetables and taking time out to sit in the garden with a cuppa have given me great pleasure. Staring up at the sky, sometimes blue with cotton-like clouds, other times misty grey with light drizzle falling into my cup, I stop to listen to the birds singing and the bees buzzing. I am calm and relaxed. The value of *rest* is crystalising in My World.

When change occurs in Our Wider World and in Your World, your Values may be challenged. You may question them. What's important to you:

- In your home country may become more, less or no longer important to you in your host country.
- Before you deal with the death of a relative may become more, less or no longer important to you afterwards.
- Before you deal with divorce or separation may become more, less or no longer important to you afterwards.
- Before you deal with ill-health may become more, less or no longer important to you afterwards.
- Before you deal with finding a job may become more, less or no longer important to you afterwards.

The importance you place on your Values can diminish or increase depending on where you are in your life and the circumstances you find yourself in. Some of your Values will remain stable throughout your life, while others will not. You may also embrace new ones.

Values Matter

When you aren't aware of your Values or aren't living in alignment with them, you may find life difficult. Violating your Values, you say and do things that don't feel right. You may feel unhappy and unfulfilled because you aren't being true to who you really are – your authentic self.

Values influence your Thoughts and Emotions. When you aren't living in accordance with your Values, your Thoughts and Emotions may be negative, pessimistic and gloomy. You may feel sad, frustrated and even angry. You may begin to sink. However, when you live in accordance with your Values, your Thoughts and Emotions will be mostly positive, optimistic and motivating. You will be content, happy and satisfied. The need to Get Leggy – see *Chapter One* – will reduce. Fear, anger, confusion, loneliness and sadness will fade away and be replaced by confidence, calmness, clarity, connections and happiness.

Values affect your relationships. When you observe the behaviours of others and take note of how they communicate and what they say, what they value in life becomes clear. Being aware of people's Values enables you to build and maintain better relationships. Think about the last time you had a misunderstanding with someone. Was it *really* a misunderstanding or was it a clash of Values? People say "I don't like him because" or "She doesn't understand me" or "I disagree with her point of view". When you don't like, don't comprehend or don't agree with someone, you dig your heels in, refusing to accept the other person's viewpoint. Your Values, in conflict with the Values of the other person, are being challenged. You are sinking. Conversely, people say "I really like him because" or "We really understand each other" or "We sing from the same hymn sheet". In agreement with the other person, you not only like what is being said but are keen to hear more. Your Values, in alignment with those of the other person, are being reinforced.

Values influence your decision-making. When you live in alignment with your Values, you set clear boundaries for yourself. You know when to say yes and when to say no. You know what you are willing to do and what you're not willing to do. You know what is acceptable to you and what isn't. Decision-making becomes a whole lot easier when you set boundaries aligned with your values.

Values impact your professional life. In my work as an HR professional, I trained to become a Personal Values Practitioner. I have designed and worked with Values-based interview questions, reviewed employee behaviours against organisational Values and trained, coached and mentored individuals to identify and work with their Values. When you realise and apply your Values, you thrive in your professional life.

In *Chapter Two* you learned that navigating culture is an enormous undertaking. When you embark on an integration journey, the most challenging aspect of the journey is recognising, understanding and coping with your host country's cultural Values. You debate whether some of your home country's Values are:

- Better than those of your host country. Experiencing a strong aversion to some of your host country's Values, you may view your host country in a less favourable light than your home country.
- Worse than those of your host country. Drawn to some of your host country's Values, you may view your host country in a more favourable light than your home country.

As you progress on your integration journey, some of your Values may change. You may begin to embrace some of your host country's Values but reject others outright. You may also begin to reject some of your home country's Values.

When you are fully aware of and live in accordance with your Values, your actions and behaviours align with who you are. As your authentic self, you are able to manage the Volatility, Uncertainty, Complexity and Ambiguity of one or more of life's most stressful situations with calmness, clarity and confidence. Swimming in crystal clear waters, your life, for the most part, flows.

Forming the essence of who you are, Values impact all aspects of your life. Values really do matter.

🏊 SWIMMING LESSON FIVE
Realise Your Values

In Swimming Lesson Five, you are being tasked with realising your Values. The lesson is in four parts. Complete all four. It may take longer than the suggested timeframes, and that's OK.

At the end of this Swimming Lesson you'll find a partially completed example.

PART ONE

Complete the sentences below. Write what springs to mind. Don't overthink. Be specific.

When things in my life flow, I am ...

When I am motivated, calm, relaxed and happy, I am ...

I care most about ...

I spend most of my money on ...

I spend most of my time ...

I am irritated, frustrated, even angry when ...

I am most proud of myself when ...

PART TWO

Reflecting on your answers in Part One, consider the repeating themes and the themes you instinctively know are important to you. Write them below.

PART THREE

Take each theme listed in Part Two one by one. Write a short paragraph about each.

Theme:

This theme is important to me because ...

Re-read the above paragraph, then below, write key words from your text, words that resonate with you and that shout *Yes, this is exactly what I Value in my life. These are my Values.*

My Value(s) related to this theme:

Remember, when you have completed one theme from Part Two, move on to the next. Continue until you have completed all themes.

You'll find space for writing your answers for two more themes below. Use this or a notebook, PC or tablet to document your answers. Once all themes have been completed, move on to Part Four.

Take the next theme listed in Part Two and write a short paragraph about it.

Theme:

This theme is important to me because ...

Re-read the above paragraph, then below, write key words from your text, words that resonate with you and that shout *Yes, this is exactly what I Value in my life. These are my Values.*

My Value(s) related to this theme:

Take the next theme listed in Part Two and write a short paragraph about it.

Theme:

This theme is important to me because ...

Re-read the above paragraph, then below, write key words from your text, words that resonate with you and that shout *Yes, this is exactly what I Value in my life. These are my Values.*

My Value(s) related to this theme:

PART FOUR

List below the Values you identified in Part Three. Re-read your list. Circle the five Values *most* important to you.

Congratulations. You have realised your Values.

Example

🏊 SWIMMING LESSON FIVE
Realise Your Values

In Swimming Lesson Five, you are being tasked with realising your Values. The lesson is in four parts. Complete all four. It may take longer than the suggested timeframes, and that's OK.

PART ONE

Complete the sentences below. Write what springs to mind. Don't overthink. Be specific.

When things in my life flow, I am ...

Gardening. Sitting in the garden, enjoying nature.
Cooking and baking with fresh ingredients.
Learning. Reading books and researching and attending courses and webinars about life abroad, health and well-being, and self-development.
Sharing my knowledge with others. The topics are the same as for learning.

When I am motivated, calm, relaxed and happy, I am ...

Gardening. Sitting in the garden, enjoying nature.
Cooking and baking with fresh ingredients.
Learning. Reading books and researching and attending courses and webinars about life abroad, health and well-being, and self-development.
Sharing my knowledge with others – through teaching, training,

mentoring and coaching. The topics are the same as for learning: life abroad, health and well-being, and self-development.
Swimming, doing yoga, walking at the beach and in the woods.

I care most about…

People being truthful, not exaggerating and not lying.
People being listened to.
People having the opportunity to have their say and to ask questions.

I spend most of my money on…

Books and personal development courses. Plants.

PART TWO

Reflecting on your answers in Part One, consider the repeating themes and the themes you instinctively know are important to you. Write them below.

Gardening. Sitting in the garden, enjoying nature.
Cooking and baking with fresh ingredients.
Learning. Reading books and researching and attending courses and webinars about life abroad, health and well-being, and self-development.
Sharing my knowledge with others. The topics are the same as for learning.
Swimming, doing yoga, walking at the beach and in the woods.
People being truthful, not exaggerating and not lying.
People being listened to.
People having the opportunity to have their say and to ask questions.

PART THREE

Take each theme listed in Part Two one by one. Write a short paragraph about each.

Theme: *Learning*

This theme is important to me because ...

I love to learn, to broaden my knowledge and to share my learning with others. I need to know the truth, to not be lied to. I like to reflect on and question what I already know.
Learning for me is about continuously improving to deliver quality in all that I do and to grow. It's about the personal development of self and others.

Re-read the above paragraph, then below, write key words from your text, words that resonate with you and that shout Yes, this is exactly what I Value in my life. These are my Values.

My Value(s) related to this theme:

Learning
Truth
Continuous Improvement
Quality
Growth

Remember, when you have completed one theme from Part Two, move on to the next. Continue until you have completed all themes.

PART FOUR

List below all the Values you identified in Part Three. Re-read your list. Circle the five Values *most* important to you.

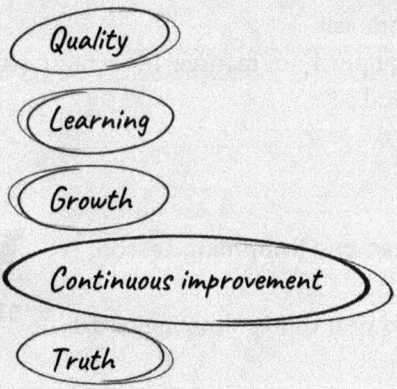

Congratulations. You have realised your Values.

Chapter Summary

In this chapter you learned ...

- When you realise and live in accordance with your Values, you are swimming in crystal clear waters, being your authentic self.
- You need to be fully aware of and embrace your Values to live a happy and fulfilled life.
- Values originate from several sources, including:
  - Your family, teachers, friends, work colleagues, and the cultures of your home and host countries.
  - Your deep-rooted beliefs.
  - A lack or a void in your life.

- Some Values remain constant during your lifetime while others do not. You may also embrace new ones and let go of others.
- Values matter. Living your Values:
  - Reduces the need to Get Leggy with negative, pessimistic and gloomy Thoughts and Emotions.
  - Enables you to build better relationships with others.
  - Enables you to understand why you may view your home country's Values more or less favourably than those of your host country and vice versa.
  - Is about being your authentic self.
  - Means you are better equipped to manage life's most stressful situations when living abroad.
- How to realise your Values.

In this chapter you have completed one Swimming Lesson.

Congratulate yourself. You've earned your third swimming medal.

Useful Resources

- Play *The Values Game.* Peter Gerrickens, Marijke Verstege, Zjev van Dun. 2003.
- Read *The Values Factor.* Dr John Demartini. 2013. Penguin Publishing Group.
- Watch *How to Determine Your Core Values.* Dr John Demartini. https://www.youtube.com/watch?v=Ptv2RQzVUuE
- Watch *What Are Your Personal Values?* Envato Tuts+ https://www.youtube.com/watch?v=NprWF3h6Yvo

A Ripple of Laughter

What do brain surgeons value?
An open mind.

Source: https://upjoke.com/open-mind-jokes

CHAPTER FOUR

Swimming Strokes: Your Strengths

"What lies behind you and what lies in front of you pales in comparison to what lies within you."

Ralph Waldo Emerson
American philosopher famous for focusing on self-reliance and non-conformity

What Are Strengths?

Strengths are:

- Your best qualities.
- What come naturally to you.
- What you enjoy doing.
- What motivate you.
- What others say you are good at.
- A part of your identity.

According to Alex Linley and Trudy Bateman in *The Strengths Profile Book*, a book I became familiar with in 2020 when I became a Strengths Profile Practitioner, Strengths comprise three aspects, namely:

1. "Performance – How well you perform when using these Strengths."
2. "Energy – How energised you are by using these Strengths."
3. "Use – How often you use these Strengths."

Books, articles or an internet search on the subject of Strengths will bring you face-to-face with list upon list of Strengths, which may include the following:

Accountability	Creativity	Humility	Perseverance
Adaptability	Curiosity	Independence	Planning
Ambition	Decision-Making	Innovation	Problem-Solving
Authenticity	Discipline	Listening	Resilience
Collaboration	Empathy	Observation	Self-belief
Compassion	Focus	Optimism	Service
Connecting	Growth	Organising	Teamwork
Courage	Honesty	Patience	Tolerance

From Where Do Strengths Originate?

Strengths originate from several sources.

Your Strengths originate mostly from your parents. However, throughout your life, you take on board the Strengths of others, such as friends, teachers and work colleagues. And, as you learn new skills and acquire new knowledge, new Strengths emerge.

In my late teens, my mum taught me to type. With practice, the countless pieces of screwed-up paper began to dwindle. Typing is one of my skills through which I realise my Strengths of continuous improvement, learning, and writing. During my university years, my tutor taught me the importance of writing short, sharp sentences. While I don't always get this right, I'm conscious of the importance of doing so. This skill has transmuted into my Strength of being an explainer.

Strengths also originate from personality traits. In 2003 I became a Thomas International Personal Profile Practitioner. The Thomas personality profiling model encompasses four aspects:

1. Dominance – adventurous, competitive and in need of a challenge.
2. Influence – persuasive, optimistic, charming and confident.
3. Steadiness – patient, easy-going and willing to help others.
4. Compliance – accurate, logical, systematic and cautious.

When you realise your personality traits, you also realise your Strengths. For example, my personality profile states, "Sue is willing to venture into the unknown in order to reach her objective." My Strengths of *courage* and *focus* are clearly visible in this single sentence.

Strengths also originate from Values. Visible through your behaviours, Values are Strengths in action. For example, in *Chapter Five* you will learn that Evgeny and Laura value humour. They laugh to release tension and anxiety. Humour, through its application, is one of their Strengths.

Strengths are also talents, your innate gifts. They are the things you simply love to do. For example, I love organising things. Everything has its place and there is a place for everything. Organising comes naturally to me. It is one of my Strengths.

Strengths Fluctuate

Some people argue that Strengths remain stable throughout life, while others argue they change. I suggest both are true. While Strengths from your childhood remain relatively constant, you will learn new ones. You may also over- and under-utilise others. Some Strengths become more or less important at different stages of your life.

Here's an example of my under-utilised strength of *service*.

> Constantly alert to the needs of others, I have regularly gone out of my way to guide, support and assist them. Service has been a key part of my work. As I'm not currently working, my Strength of service is under-utilised. I have no doubt, however, that when I return to work in the future, service will once again come to the fore.

Here's an example of my over-utilised strength of *focus*.

> Frowning at inefficiencies and time-wasting, I have always been a stickler for doing things well and delivering on time. Placing unnecessary pressure on myself, I have overworked. My energy levels became depleted. Furthermore, I recognise that being too focused has resulted in missed opportunities.

When change occurs in Our Wider World and in Your World, your Strengths may be challenged and you may subsequently question them. The Strengths important to you:

- In your home country may become more, less or no longer important to you in your host country.
- Before you deal with the death of a relative may become more, less or no longer important to you afterwards.
- Before you deal with divorce or separation may become more, less or no longer important to you afterwards.
- Before you deal with ill-health may become more, less or no longer important to you afterwards.
- Before you deal with finding a job may become more, less or no longer important to you afterwards.

The importance you place on your Strengths can diminish or increase depending on where you are in your life and the circumstances you find yourself in. Some of your Strengths will remain stable throughout your life, while others will not. You may also embrace new ones.

Strengths Matter

According to James Clear in *Atomic Habits*, realising your Strengths is about knowing where to spend your time and energy, specifically knowing "which types of opportunities to look for and which types of challenges to avoid". When you realise and utilise your Strengths, your life will mostly flow. Conversely, when you aren't aware of your Strengths, you'll likely be utilising skills and knowledge and embracing Strengths incompatible with who you are. Your life may be unnecessarily difficult.

Strengths influence your Thoughts and Emotions. When you aren't utilising your Strengths, your Thoughts and Emotions may be negative, pessimistic and gloomy. You may feel sad, frustrated and sometimes angry. You may begin to sink. Conversely, when you utilise your Strengths, your Thoughts and Emotions will be mostly positive, optimistic and motivating. You'll be happy, content and satisfied. The need to Get Leggy, a tool you became familiar with in *Chapter One*, diminishes. Fear, anger, confusion, loneliness and sadness fade away, replaced by confidence, calmness, clarity, connections and happiness.

Strengths affect your relationships. When you observe the behaviours of others and take note of their communication style and what they say, their Strengths become evident. When you support others with your own Strengths and vice versa, you build and maintain better relationships.

Strengths show up in all aspects of your professional life. As an HR professional, I have designed and worked with Strength-based interview questions, performance reviews and development plans and have trained, coached and mentored individuals to realise their Strengths. When you apply your Strengths in your professional life, you thrive.

As mentioned earlier, when you realise and utilise your Strengths, your life, for the most part, flows. Utilising your most appropriate Strengths, your best swimming strokes, you calmly and confidently manage the inevitable Volatility, Uncertainty, Complexity and Ambiguity that arises when faced with one or more of life's most stressful situations.

Strengths impact all aspects of your life. Strengths really do matter.

SWIMMING LESSON SIX
Realise Your Strengths

In Swimming Lesson Six, you are being tasked with realising your Strengths. The lesson is in four parts. Complete all four. It may take longer than the suggested timeframes, and that's OK.

At the end of this Swimming Lesson you'll find a partially completed example.

PART ONE

Complete the sentences below. Write what springs to mind. Don't overthink. Be specific.

When I am performing at my best, enjoying what I am doing and feeling truly alive, I am ...

SWIMMING STROKES: YOUR STRENGTHS

Things that come naturally to me, that I do without thinking are ...

Others tell me I am good at ...

PART TWO

Reflecting on your answers in Part One, consider the repeating themes and themes you instinctively know you are good at and enjoy doing. Write them below.

PART THREE

Take each theme listed in Part Two one by one. Write a short paragraph about each.

Theme:

I am good at and enjoy this because ...

Re-read the above paragraph, then below, write key words from your text, words that resonate with you and that shout *Yes, this is one of my Strengths*.

My Strength(s) related to this theme:

If you'd like some help identifying your Strengths from the key words, visit The Strengths Profile dictionary here:
https://files.strengthsprofile.com/Deployable/LocalizableResources/en-gb/Resources/Strengths_Profile_Definitions.pdf

Remember, when you have completed one theme from Part Two, move on to the next. Continue until you have completed all themes.

You'll find space for writing your answers for two more themes below. Use this or a notebook, PC or tablet to document your answers. Once all themes have been completed, move on to Part Four.

Take the next theme listed in Part Two and write a short paragraph about it.

Theme:

I am good at and enjoy this because ...

Re-read the above paragraph, then below, write key words from your text, words that resonate with you and that shout *Yes, this is one of my Strengths*.

My Strength(s) related to this theme:

SWIMMING STROKES: YOUR STRENGTHS

Take the next theme listed in Part Two and write a short paragraph about it.

Theme:

I am good at and enjoy this because ...

Re-read the above paragraph, then below, write key words from your text, words that resonate with you and that shout *Yes, this is one of my Strengths*.

My Strength(s) related to this theme:

PART FOUR

List below the Strengths you identified in Part Three. Re-read your list. Circle the five Strengths *most* important to you.

Congratulations. You have realised your Strengths.

Example

🏊 SWIMMING LESSON SIX
Realise Your Strengths

In Swimming Lesson Six, you are being tasked with realising your Strengths. The lesson is in four parts. Complete all four. It may take longer than the suggested timeframes, and that's OK.

PART ONE

Complete the sentences below. Write what springs to mind. Don't overthink. Be specific.

When I am performing at my best, enjoying what I am doing and feeling truly alive, I am ...

Delivering presentations and workshops. Sharing my knowledge and experiences. Learning. Reading. Writing. Training. Mentoring. Coaching. Serving others. Organising. Improving things. Cooking. Baking. Gardening.

Things that come naturally to me, that I do without thinking are ...

Gardening. Cooking. Baking. Listening. Improving things. Organising. Treating people equally. Giving feedback. Giving others the opportunity to be heard. Taking ownership of what I am accountable for. Delivering what I promise.

Others tell me I am good at ...

Listening. Serving and being an advocate for others.

Solving problems. Building rapport. Making others laugh. Detail. Being pragmatic, optimistic, focused and organised. Presenting. Never giving up. Taking pride in and producing quality work.

PART TWO

Reflecting on your answers in Part One, consider the repeating themes and the themes you instinctively know you are good at and enjoy doing. Write them below.

Training. Mentoring. Coaching. Presenting. Organising. Improving things. Equal treatment. Accountability. Delivering what I promise. Listening. Researching. Serving others. Problem-solving. Sense of humour. Pragmatic. Approachable. Focused. Optimistic. Determination. Quality. Courage.

PART THREE

Take each theme listed in Part Two one by one. Write a short paragraph about each.

Theme: *Training*

I am good at and enjoy this because ...

I'm sharing my knowledge and experiences with others, enabling them to grow. I am being of service to others.

Re-read the above paragraph, then below, write key words from your text, words that resonate with you and that shout *Yes, this is one of my Strengths*.

My Strength(s) related to this theme:

Growth

Service

Learning

Remember, when you have completed one theme from Part Two, move on to the next. Continue until you have completed all themes.

PART FOUR

List below the Strengths you identified in Part Three. Re-read your list. Circle the five Strengths *most* important to you.

(Quality)

(Growth)

Being an Organiser

(Learning)

(Pragmatism)

(Service)

Congratulations. You have realised your Strengths.

Not Forgetting Weaknesses

I could be flippant and say, forget about your Weaknesses. They serve no purpose, right? Wrong. Weaknesses tell a story about what you are not good at and what you don't enjoy. Realising your Weaknesses is just as important as realising your Strengths.

While there may be times when you have no choice but to use one or more of your Weaknesses, I recommend keeping their use to a minimum, accepting – at best – a satisfactory level of performance. When you avoid using or limit the use of your Weaknesses you can:

- Focus your time and energy on developing your Strengths. For example, at school it was compulsory to study at least one science. I disliked sciences but chose chemistry. Importantly, I directed my time and energy to studying other subjects, subjects I enjoyed and was good at.
- Utilise Strengths to compensate for Weaknesses. "Tell me about your Strengths and Weaknesses" is the one interview question we all expect, yet dread. Realising which of your Strengths compensate for your Weaknesses is a great way to answer this question. For example, one of my Weaknesses is competitiveness. But rather than competing with others to succeed, I choose to use my Strengths of self-motivation and continuous improvement. I compete with myself.
- Seek assistance from others who have Strengths in your areas of Weakness and vice versa.

🏊 SWIMMING LESSON SEVEN
Strengths to Overcome Weaknesses

In Swimming Lesson Seven, you are being tasked with understanding your Weaknesses and documenting which of your Strengths can compensate for these. The lesson is in three parts. Complete all three.

PART ONE

Complete the sentence below. Write what springs to mind. Don't overthink. Be specific.

Things I am not good at and don't enjoy are ...

PART TWO

Reflect on your answer in Part One, then below, write key words from your text, words that resonate with you and that shout *Yes, this is one of my Weaknesses*.

PART THREE

List no more than three Weaknesses from Part Two. Identify which of your Strengths (detailed in Swimming Lesson Six) compensate for these and how.

Weaknesses	Compensatory Strengths and How
For example:	*For example:*
Being Competitive	Service – I strive to exceed the needs of others through my own quality standards as opposed to those of others.

SWIMMING STROKES: YOUR STRENGTHS

Weaknesses	Compensatory Strengths and How

Chapter Summary

In this chapter you learned ...

- When you realise and utilise your Strengths:
    - you are swimming your best swimming strokes.
    - your life mostly flows.
- Strengths originate from:
    - Family, friends, teachers and work colleagues.
    - Skills and knowledge.
    - Personality traits.
    - Values.
    - Talents.

- Some Strengths remain stable over time, others not. You may embrace new Strengths and let go of others during your lifetime.
- Strengths matter. When utilising your Strengths:
  - The need to Get Leggy with negative, pessimistic and gloomy Thoughts and Emotions diminishes.
  - You build better relationships with others.
  - Your professional life thrives.
  - You are better able to manage life's most stressful situations abroad.
- Strengths can compensate for your Weaknesses.

In this chapter you have completed two Swimming Lessons.

Congratulate yourself. You've earned your fourth swimming medal.

Useful Resources

- Complete a *free* Strengths Profile here: https://www.strengthsprofile.com/en-gb/products/free
- Read *Now, Discover Your Strengths.* Don Clifton. 2020. Gallup Press.
- Read *The Strengths Book.* Sally Bibb. 2017. LID Publishing Ltd.
- Read *The Strengths Profile Book.* Alex Linley and Trudy Bateman. 2018. Capp Press.
- Watch *Strengths and Challenges.* Job Journey CanAssist. https://www.youtube.com/watch?v=3Aem-dluC80
- Watch *The Simple Way to Find STRENGTH in Your WEAKNESS.* Simon Sinek. https://www.youtube.com/watch?v=FTPmW1vP3JE

A Ripple of Laughter

What did the ocean ask the whales to do?
Show their mussels.

PART THREE

SINK THEN SWIM DURING LIFE'S MOST STRESSFUL SITUATIONS

> "Sometimes everything hits you all at once. You lose a relationship, change jobs, old friends go and new friends come. It's up one day and down the next. You have it all together on Monday and by Thursday you don't have a clue. Life is one big wave and all we can do is flow, grow and adapt."

Sylvester McNutt
American author, podcaster and public speaker

CHAPTER FIVE

Sink Then Swim Living Abroad: The Stories

"Living in a foreign culture is like playing a game you've never played before and for which the rules haven't been explained very well. The challenge is to enjoy the game without missing too many plays, learning the rules and developing skills as you go along."

Robert L Kohls
Founding member of the Society for Intercultural Education, Training and Research (SIETAR)

The Foundation of Your Life Abroad

"Resettling is one of the most stressful 'life events' because it affects every aspect of our lives, including our social networks, our personal and professional identities, our economic circumstances and every one of our daily routines," Diane Lemieux and Anne Parker tell us in *The Mobile Life*, a book that looks at ways in which to build a successful life abroad.

When you decided to live abroad you signed up for concentrated, accelerated and extensive change, change laden with Volatility, Uncertainty, Complexity and Ambiguity. You didn't expect everything in your host country to be the same as your home country, did you? You knew you would come face-to-face with difference.

In your home country you're a big fish in a small pond. You know how things work and who to call for help and support. It's comfortable and, for the most part, it's easy. Conversely, in your host country you're a small fish in a big pond.

You don't know how everything works and you likely have no one to call on for help and support. It's uncomfortable and far from easy.

Your host country's cultural waters swell and crash with challenges on the one hand yet lap and glisten with opportunities on the other. This is the foundation on which you will build your life abroad and on which you will handle other stressful situations, including death, divorce and separation, ill-health and finding a job.

Acutely aware of the foundation on which our lives abroad are built, I and others I know regularly reflect on our experiences. In the living abroad stories that follow, Anna, Evgeny, Hortense, Laura, Matilde, Nicole and Pauline share how they handled the differences between their home and host countries. We'll take a look at the circumstances in which they sank and then swam, what they learned from their experiences, and how they Got Leggy with their negative, pessimistic and gloomy Thoughts and Emotions. Then finally, we'll see how their Values and Strengths came to the fore.

THE LIVING ABROAD STORIES

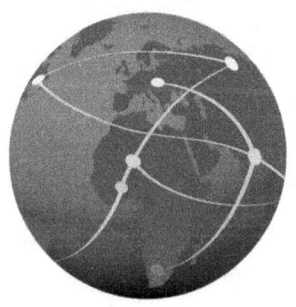

Anna
Evgeny
Hortense
Laura
Matilde
Nicole
Pauline

1. WHERE'S HOME?
ANNA'S LIVING ABROAD STORY

Living abroad is all Anna knows. She left Spain at just six months old when her father relocated for work. Her subsequent relocations have been to study or related to her husband's work. She has lived in nine countries (Belgium, France, the Netherlands, Nigeria, Norway, Peru, Sweden, Thailand and the USA), and despite understanding the integration journey inside out, transitioning between countries hasn't always been easy. Anna speaks several languages and is currently living in Sweden.

Anna **SINKS**

Baptism of fire
Once again living away from family and friends and with her partner on his own integration journey, Anna was juggling almost everything alone. The support network she had developed in her previous host country was no longer on her doorstep. She barely knew her new location, the people or the language, and when she asked for help, she regularly encountered locals who refused to communicate in any language other than their own. This Volatile experience repeated itself every time she relocated. With her confidence dented and no one to turn to, overwhelm and exhaustion set in. She became hostile and critical towards the locals and her host country.

Language
Although Anna was confident about her language capabilities, she became aware that learning languages can be more Complex than she had envisaged. Differences may seem small but they can be big enough to create issues. Many words look the same but the pronunciation and sometimes the meaning can be different. Knowing Norwegian was one thing, but understanding Swedish was another matter.

Socialising
Anna's husband was a homebird. From her previous relocations she had learned that staying home would hinder her integration and bring about feelings of loneliness. She needed to get out of the house, to connect and socialise with others. This didn't come naturally to her, however. She was shy, an introvert who needed to push herself out of her comfort zone. Making new friends took time, often longer than she would have liked.

... and then **SWIMS**

Behaviours
Observing and copying the behaviours of the locals proved to be a safe and modest way for Anna to learn about and adapt to her host country. She would also speak with the locals to learn more and sometimes gained new friends by doing so. She is proud of who she has become, now referring to herself as a social extrovert.

Do your homework
"Any information you obtain before you relocate is useful," Anna stressed. These days the internet is a great source, as is speaking with other internationals living in your soon-to-be host country. Gathering information about the cost of living, safety and security, further education and more, gave Anna insight into what lay ahead. This lessened any Uncertainty surrounding her move, calmed her nerves and increased her confidence. As the saying goes, 'forewarned is forearmed'.

Family of friends
Anna immersed herself in the local community. Joining networking and hobby groups enabled her to develop friendships with both locals and internationals. The friendships she has all over the world have become her 'little family of friends' who refer to her as the glue in their relationship. "If you hadn't written every month, called and visited me, I don't think we would still be in contact," one friend said. Anna is similarly grateful to her friends who have helped her survive the numerous challenges she has encountered living in nine different countries.

Feeling at home
Anna has developed an interesting perspective on the word 'home'. Home is often referred to as a physical place. But having lived abroad almost all her life, for Anna, home has become the extent to which she feels comfortable in her own skin and feels at home in her host country – the degree of compatibility between the beliefs and Values she has developed from living in different countries and those of her current host country.

> "When you live abroad you have one foot in at least two countries. It can be difficult to know where home is."
> **Anna in Sweden**

Anna's Living Abroad Learnings

Anna's story highlights how living abroad brings Volatility, Uncertainty, Complexity and Ambiguity to the fore. Her experiences highlight how important it is to:

- Have a do-it-yourself mentality yet recognise you need support, especially in the beginning. You can't do everything alone.
- Realise that languages are different even when two or more countries use the same or similar words.
- Push yourself out of your comfort zone to connect and socialise with others.
- Observe and copy the behaviours of locals to learn about and adapt to your host country's culture.
- Research your host country before emigrating.
- Recognise that home can be more than just a physical place.
- Keep in contact with friends wherever you and they live in the world.
- Develop new friendships by joining networking and hobby organisations.

Anna Got Leggy

Anna viewed most of the challenges she faced as opportunities to push herself forward – to swim. Any negative, pessimistic and gloomy Thoughts and Emotions that arose were consequently quashed. When asked how she managed confusion, fear and loneliness, she said:

- **From Confusion to Clarity** – "Any information I got from the internet and from others about the host country was useful."

- **From Fear to Confidence** – "I was an introvert, but when I stepped out of my comfort zone, I became a social extrovert."

- **From Loneliness to Connections** – "I connected with others and gained a little family of friends by networking and joining hobby groups."

Anna's Values and Strengths

Anna's story highlights the Values and Strengths she draws on to manage her life abroad. They include:

- **Connections** – Anna joined networking and hobby groups to make new friends. She has worked tirelessly to develop new friendships and maintain existing ones wherever she and her friends live in the world. She also observed and copied the behaviours of locals to learn about and adapt to her host country's culture.

- **Pragmatism** – Anna researched her host country in advance, and when she arrived she immersed herself in the local community. She knew socialising was critical to integrating.

- **Resilience** – Anna stepped out of her comfort zone, joining networking and hobby groups to make friends and avoid feeling lonely. She was an introvert but now refers to herself as a social extrovert.

2. IT'S THE SMALL THINGS THAT MATTER: EVGENY'S LIVING ABROAD STORY

"I was at breaking point. It wasn't safe and it wasn't right," Evgeny said, referring to the war between Russia and Ukraine. With little hesitation, he began looking for opportunities to leave his home country, Russia. Turkey wasn't the destination he had in mind, but it was a start. At the time of writing, he has lived in Turkey for almost two years and is within days of fulfilling his dream of working in Europe. Evgeny speaks three languages.

Evgeny **SINKS**

Expect the unexpected

Evgeny came face-to-face with Uncertainty, Complexity and Ambiguity as cultural inconsistencies began playing out within minutes of arriving in Turkey.

It was late in the evening when Evgeny and his family arrived in Istanbul. "Two minutes, my friend," the polite and friendly taxi marshal said repeatedly. Forty-five minutes later, their taxi arrived. Patience, tolerance and indirectness, prominent features of Turkish culture, were not something Evgeny possessed at this time. It had been a long day. He and his family were exhausted.

At the hotel, his children were put to bed, but their sleep was instantly disturbed. It was obvious what it was, but the Muslim call to prayer still came as a surprise. "How can people be expected to sleep through this?" Evgeny said to his wife as they looked at each other in dismay.

Evgeny's initial request to open a bank account was declined. Returning the following day, greeted by the same bank clerk sitting on the same chair, his application was approved. The situation was both confusing and infuriating.

Food glorious food

"Meh. Meaty, fatty food steeped in spices," he said. Food choices were not to his liking. Restaurants serving steak, sushi and Italian dishes, food he was used to and enjoyed, were over a thirty-minute drive away. Reminiscing about chatting with friends while having a meal in the heart of St Petersburg, Evgeny was missing his home city.

Temporary move?

Evgeny knew the importance of learning the language, but his mind was elsewhere, focused on securing employment in Europe. Envisaging the stay in Turkey would be short-lived, he and his family lived out of unpacked suitcases. Consequently, he learned only a handful of Turkish words.

... and then SWIMS

Connections
Evgeny lived in a condominium complex with three other Russian families. He has no doubt the rock-solid friendships formed during their time together will remain so for a long time, despite them now living in different countries.

Out and about, Evgeny engaged in small talk with the locals, shop owners, his doctor and the bank manager. Feeling comfortable around Turkish people, he embraced their friendliness and approachability. "I find them easy to relate to and to read, somewhat like Russians," he said.

Everything stops for tea
"You can't interrupt tea time," Evgeny said. The bank clerks stopped working as soon as a tray of teacups appeared, and normal service resumed only when all cups were empty. Evgeny found this cultural quirk entertaining. Smiling and sometimes tittering while waiting in line to be served, he realised he was getting used to the 'everything stops for tea' moment.

Paperwork
"She's a bureaucratic monster and I'm grateful she is." Evgeny laughed. He was referring to his wife who, before leaving Russia, had made a copy of official documents and, to ensure that money could be easily transferred when necessary, had organised a power of attorney. Having a file full of personal documents ready for the Turkish Consul proved crucial when applying for their residence permits.

Simple pleasures of nature
Sitting at the embankment in the midst of winter, people-watching and drinking tea, and walking in the forest admiring the lush green pine trees was calming. Evgeny was at peace in nature. And exploring the vastness and beauty of Turkey enabled him to remain focused on his dream of one day working in Europe.

> "It's the small things in life that matter – food, tea, nature, habits and laughter. I also changed the colour of my hair. It was fun and it felt good."
> **Evgeny in Turkey**

Evgeny's Living Abroad Learnings

Evgeny's story highlights how living abroad brings Volatility, Uncertainty, Complexity and Ambiguity to the fore. His experiences highlight how important it is to:

- Recognise and interpret cultural norms.
- Understand that persistence is often necessary to get the basics in place. For example, opening a bank account.
- Appreciate that local food may not be to your liking.
- Realise that a temporary move may become long-term.
- Learn the language.
- Appreciate friendships.
- Connect with locals.
- Smile and laugh at the unusual.
- Appreciate that nature is an enabler of calmness and focus.
- Have copies of official documents.
- Set up a power of attorney in your home country.
- Remain focused on why you are emigrating.

Evgeny Got Leggy

Evgeny viewed most of the challenges he faced as opportunities to push himself forward – to swim. Any negative, pessimistic and gloomy Thoughts and Emotions that arose were consequently quashed. When asked how he managed anger, confusion and fear, he said:

- **From Anger to Calm** – "I was agitated having to wait for our pre-booked taxi, but, on reflection, the friendliness of the marshal helped calm my nerves."

- **From Confusion to Clarity** – "Knowing about Turkish inconsistencies in advance would have helped, but in the end, I learned to accept them."

- **From Fear to Confidence** – "Leaving Russia during wartime was both scary and distressing. Turkey became an important stepping stone to realising my dream of living in Europe."

Evgeny's Values and Strengths

Evgeny's story highlights the Values and Strengths he draws on to manage his life abroad. They include:

- **Courage** – Evgeny left Russia with no guarantees and under a cloud of Uncertainty.

- **Humour** – Evgeny chose to giggle and smile at some Turkish habits, including the bank clerks' tea routines. He also laughed when referring to his wife as a bureaucratic monster.

- **Perseverance** – Undeterred by the initial 'no' response to opening a bank account, Evgeny returned the following day to get what he desperately needed. Being in nature also helped him remain focused on his dream of working in Europe.

3. UNWRAP THE *WHY* OF YOUR HOST COUNTRY'S CULTURE: HORTENSE'S LIVING ABROAD STORY

Hortense had dreamt of living in Europe from a young age. In her late teens, she moved to France to study, but with job vacancies few and far between when she graduated, she returned to the USA. Years later, after researching several countries of interest and having completed a master's degree that could help her secure employment in Europe, she began a scholarship in Norway. Over a period of twenty-three years, Hortense has lived in five countries (France, Germany, Namibia, Norway and Serbia). Currently living in Norway, she speaks four languages. She has always relocated alone.

Hortense **SINKS**

Behaviours and communication
Hortense's American ways and opinions have sometimes been viewed with criticism and other times dismissed outright. "I was no longer a trusted source of information," she said. The locals didn't appreciate that things were done differently in the USA. She sensed locals viewed her as a complainer, someone who was attacking their culture. Attempting to fit in to her current host country, Norway, has, at times, been exhausting.

Food glorious food
"The absence of cheap doughnuts, dill pickles and take-out Chinese food makes me grumpy," she said. Home comforts readily available in the USA have not always been available in her host countries.

Language
Hortense knew learning the language was important. Making sense of product labels in grocery stores was, in the beginning, no easy task. It made her brain ache. Her progress was further hindered by locals who repeatedly switched to English when hearing her accent. She became frustrated and, at times, annoyed by her slow progress.

Protecting yourself
Two men approached Hortense at a cash machine in Namibia. "Hey, whitey, what are you doing here?" they shouted. Sensing she was in a potentially dangerous situation, she collected her money and walked calmly and quickly away. "I believe those guys thought I was an easy target, possessing money they possibly didn't have. Perhaps they also wanted to show their power. Namibia had, after all, been independent from Apartheid for just eight years," she said. Nothing had prepared her to know what to do in this Volatile, intimidating and frightening situation.

... and then **SWIMS**

Behaviours
Figuring out the *why* of her host country's culture, *why people do what they do*, was a Complex task, yet it proved to be a real motivator. "Ask a Brit why they queue in an orderly fashion and why they drive on the left, and they probably won't be able to tell you," Hortense said. After literally bumping into Norwegians in the street more than she dare admit, she told other international friends living in Norway about her predicament. Norwegians, they explained, value their space. A glance of the eye means you need to move out of their way. Knowing this and subsequently observing and analysing the behaviours of the locals helped Hortense understand why the locals do what they do.

Language
Learning the language and specifically where the emphasis is placed in both written and spoken communication provided further clarity to what was important to the locals. Further, it came with an added bonus. After passing the state integration language exam, Hortense was granted Norwegian citizenship. She was free to live and work within the EU. "They can't kick me out," she said, smiling.

Networking
Searching for a greater understanding of the different ways of doing things, Hortense joined international networking groups. Within these groups, a level of frustration existed. Integrating was, for many, not easy. Sharing stories with like-minded people made her realise she had been viewing things from her own cultural perspective. What's more, her feelings of loneliness dissipated as she developed new friendships.

> "Understand why the locals do what they do. You are the outsider. You need to adapt, not them."
> **Hortense in Norway**

Hortense's Living Abroad Learnings

Hortense's story highlights how living abroad brings Volatility, Uncertainty, Complexity and Ambiguity to the fore. Her experiences highlight how important it is to:

- Research the economy and educational requirements of the host country.
- Appreciate that locals may not be able to relate to the ways of your home country.
- Understand that food items readily available in your home country may not be available in your host country.
- Appreciate that language learning can be slow, especially when locals switch to English.
- Be aware of and prepare for potentially threatening situations.
- Recognise that you, not the locals, need to adapt.
- Use your observation and analytical skills to deduce why people do what they do.
- Learn the language.
- Identify where the emphasis is placed in both spoken and written communication to appreciate what's important to the locals.
- Join international networking groups to better understand cultural differences and to appreciate that you are not alone on your integration journey.

Hortense Got Leggy

Hortense viewed most of the challenges she faced as opportunities to push herself forward – to swim. Any negative, pessimistic and gloomy Thoughts and Emotions that arose were consequently quashed. When asked how she managed confusion, fear and loneliness, she said:

- **From Confusion to Clarity** – "To understand the culture you need to observe and analyse behaviours and listen to what the locals are saying."

- **From Fear to Confidence** – "I found inner courage to walk quickly and calmly away from what was a potentially dangerous situation."

- **From Loneliness to Connections** – "The more I interacted with others, the more I realised I wasn't alone with my integration challenges."

Hortense's Values and Strengths

Hortense's story highlights the Values and Strengths she draws on to manage her life abroad. They include:

- **Courage** – Hortense wasn't afraid to point out to locals that some things are done differently beyond their country's border. She also walked calmly yet quickly away from a potentially threatening situation.

- **Perseverance** – Hortense researched the economy and the educational requirements of several countries before deciding which country to relocate to. She also completed a master's degree to help her secure employment in Europe.

- **Willingness to Learn** – Hortense found answers to why locals do what they do by learning the language and sharing stories with other internationals at networking events. She also identified where the emphasis is placed in languages by observing and listening to the locals.

4. PARALLEL TRACKS: LAURA'S LIVING ABROAD STORY

Laura loves the challenge of starting over. "One suitcase and off I go," she said. She has relocated for study or family-related reasons and has always done so alone. Originally from Croatia, she has lived in four countries (Norway, Russia, Spain and the UK) over a period of ten years. She speaks five languages and has repatriated six times.

Laura **SINKS**

Behaviours and communication
Laura was frustrated and confused by some aspects of Russian culture. Ambiguity was a big issue – the way business appointments were conducted, for example, or the different communication styles. Appointments could start late and run over until all agenda items were addressed. Communication was direct, with yes and no answers, but these answers could sometimes be softened to save face.

Cultural diversity
Laura was emotionally affected by the visible differences in Moscow. While in awe of the splendour of the Golden Mile, the Kremlin and Red Square, she became distressed when she saw the homeless wandering aimlessly through areas of dilapidated housing.

Few foreigners
Laura felt comfortable around the open and friendly Spaniards but missed the buzz of working in an international environment. It was the year 2000, and there were few international businesses in Madrid. Networking with other foreigners was rare.

Incompatible
"Norway was not for me," she said. It felt like she was living on parallel tracks. On the one hand, she attempted to remain true to who she is, while on the other, she tried to get to grips with Norway's cultural habits. When the tracks crossed, she felt confused, frustrated and lonely. Life in Norway was far from easy – it was Complex. Laura felt she was losing sight of who she is as she adapted to Norwegian ways.

... and then SWIMS

Become a tourist
In Russia and Spain, Laura lived the life of a tourist. "When you live in a large country you are exposed to diverse cultural experiences and you escape small country mentality," she said. In Madrid, she enjoyed hopping from museum to museum in the Golden Triangle of Art and socialising with friendly Spaniards in El Retiro Park. After enjoying paella or tapas and a glass of sangria while chatting with the locals in an open-air café, she'd sometimes take a short siesta. In Moscow, she was moved by the large avenues, urban parks and the famous Bolshoi ballet. She was also grateful for the ample and cheap supply of gas, especially during the extremely cold winter months.

Employment
Laura uses her language skills in her work. "Without language, you can't communicate with the locals, and you may have problems finding a job." In England not only was her English valued, but her qualifications and experience were too. Finding work was easy compared with some other countries.

Focused networking
Laura was appalled by internationals who made no attempt to learn the language, didn't interact with the natives and yet spoke negatively about their host country. Refusing to become part of this community, she developed friendships with locals and open-minded internationals at networking events. With these friends, she was able to be her true, authentic self.

Laughter
"Humour is a great coping mechanism," she said. Laughing at some of the cultural peculiarities in a light-hearted way helped release inner tensions. In Norway, buying alcohol is ridiculously expensive and can only be bought in the state-owned stores called Vinmonopolet. Excessive queues form prior to holiday periods when these stores close. In Spain, she watched the craziness of La Tomatina, the annual tomato fight. Streets became rivers of red pulp as strangers squashed tomatoes in each other's faces.

> "Aspects of the local culture may be somewhat or wholly incompatible with who you are. Stay true to your authentic self while adapting."
> **Laura in Croatia**

Laura's Living Abroad Learnings

Laura's story highlights how living abroad brings Volatility, Uncertainty, Complexity and Ambiguity to the fore. Her experiences highlight how important it is to:

- Recognise that some behaviours and communication styles may be difficult to relate to.
- Realise that international organisations may not exist in some countries.
- Be honest with yourself when a culture is not right for you.
- Remain true to your authentic self while adapting to a new culture, even though this may bring about feelings of incompatibility.
- Realise that cities can be diverse.
- Become a tourist to learn about the country's culture.
- Recognise that language plays a crucial role in securing employment.
- Appreciate that your qualifications and experience may be valued in some countries but not in others.
- Laugh at cultural quirks.
- Avoid internationals who are critical of your host country.
- Network with locals and open-minded internationals.

Laura Got Leggy

Laura viewed most of the challenges she faced as opportunities to push herself forward – to swim. Any negative, pessimistic and gloomy Thoughts and Emotions that arose were consequently quashed. When asked how she managed anger, loneliness and sadness, she said:

- **From Anger to Calm** – "The poverty in Moscow was disturbing, but I admired the beauty of the city's architecture."

- **From Loneliness to Connections** – "I avoided foreigners who complained about my host country. I joined networking groups instead, where I met like-minded internationals and open-minded locals."

- **From Sadness to Happiness** – "The lack of foreigners in the workplace in Spain was disappointing but I was content embracing the Spanish ways."

Laura's Values and Strengths

Laura's story highlights the Values and Strengths she draws on to manage her life abroad. They include:

- **Connections** – Laura became a tourist to explore her host country and, while doing so, socialised with locals. She also attended networking events to develop friendships with locals and open-minded internationals.

- **Humour** – Laura laughed at some of the cultural peculiarities in Norway and Spain.

- **Integrity** – Laura never lost sight of who she is despite understanding the importance of getting to grips with and adapting to her host country's culture.

5. MISSING OUT: MATILDE'S LIVING ABROAD STORY

Matilde revels in the abundance of learning opportunities living abroad brings. Her first relocation, to Cambridge, England, was to practise her English language skills. Ghana, a later move, satisfied her curiosity about living in Africa. Originally from Italy, at the time of writing Matilde is commuting between her home in Brussels, Belgium, and her work in Ghana. She speaks four languages and has lived in five countries (Belgium, Germany, Ghana, Mozambique and the UK) over a period of ten years. She has always relocated alone.

Matilde **SINKS**

Family and friends
Matilde confessed that making connections in Germany and the UK was difficult. The locals had their own circle of friends. This, along with her being an introvert, brought feelings of loneliness to the surface. Matilde missed her family and friends back home and still does. While some have visited her abroad, she has become the person who visits them. She has found this hard. During the Covid-19 Pandemic, her niece was born, but travel restrictions prevented Matilde from flying home. This made her feel like she was missing out.

Food, glorious food
Replicating Italian dishes has been challenging. When fruit and vegetables grow without sufficient sunshine, they don't taste the same. Matilde craves Italian tomatoes. "With olive oil and a sprinkle of salt, they make a delicious salad," she said.

Language nuances
Matilde loves languages. However, over the years, she has discovered that language learning has two layers. First, there are the words and grammar, and second, language nuances. While she now speaks more English than her mother tongue, Italian, she is sometimes unsure if the English are sincere, polite or downright rude. Interpreting the real meaning of what people say can be confusing and irritating. "It's a real brain challenge – Complex," she said.

Safe areas
From the moment Matilde sets foot in a new country, she goes running. For her, running equals routines and normality. "I don't care where I run, I just need to run," she said. But some countries have no-go areas, and in the Belgian winters, the days are short. This has made the simple exercise of running Volatile and Uncertain. Subsequently, Matilde reaches out to the locals to ask where it's safe to run.

... and then SWIMS

Accommodation
Finding a place to live can be a challenge. However, in the UK, Matilde found the perfect solution. Renting a room in a shared house was cheaper than renting a place on her own, plus she wasn't tied to a long-term contract. She could move out at short notice, something she needed to do when the Covid-19 Pandemic hit.

Diversity
"It's a fake environment where almost everyone's a foreigner," said Matilde, referring to Brussels. Theatre shows, street musicians and a different language being spoken on almost every street corner demonstrate the diversity of the city. But Matilde is in her element using her language skills when talking with other internationals in this multicultural city.

Nature's gift
Matilde loves working in Africa. The warm climates and sea air are both uplifting and calming. Running in the Sonian Forest in Brussels, taking in the beauty of the beech and oak trees standing tall above her head, has a similar effect. "Being in nature is excellent for your health and well-being," she said.

Strangers
"People jump to your rescue before you even realise you need assistance," Matilde said, referring to the friendly Africans she encountered in her work. People are emotional beings, and when you connect with others, you can always find something you have in common. She initiates random conversations with strangers, asking for directions even if she already knows where she is going. Any feelings of loneliness subsequently dissipate.

> "Locals have their own circle of friends.
> You need to grow your own circle too."
> **Matilde in Ghana**

Matilde's Living Abroad Learnings

Matilde's story highlights how living abroad brings Volatility, Uncertainty, Complexity and Ambiguity to the fore. Her experiences highlight how important it is to:

- Appreciate that establishing relationships with locals can be difficult.
- Recognise that relationships with family and friends back home change.
- Realise you may not always be able to return home when you want to.
- Appreciate that food may taste different.
- Interpret language nuances.
- Acknowledge that your mother tongue may take second place to another language.
- Establish routines from the outset.
- Understand where any no-go areas are.
- Rent a room in a shared house to save money and to give flexibility to move out at short notice.
- Recognise the diversity of some cities where it may feel like there are more internationals than natives.
- Be in nature to experience uplifting and calming feelings.
- Recognise the benefits of connecting with strangers.

Matilde Got Leggy

Matilde viewed most of the challenges she faced as opportunities to push herself forward – to swim. Any negative, pessimistic and gloomy Thoughts and Emotions that arose were consequently quashed. When asked how she managed fear, loneliness and sadness, she said:

- **From Fear to Confidence** – "My quality of life improved when I found safe areas in which to run."

- **From Loneliness to Connections** – "My feelings of loneliness receded when I spoke with strangers, even if I just asked for directions."

- **From Sadness to Happiness** – "I encouraged my family and friends back home to visit me to experience my life abroad. Wherever I live I find a way to develop new friendships."

Matilde's Values and Strengths

Matilde's story highlights the Values and Strengths she draws on to manage her life abroad. They include:

- **Adaptability** – Matilde initiated conversations with strangers. She also used her language skills to speak with other internationals.

- **Pragmatism** – Keen to maintain her routines, Matilde spoke with locals to learn where she could run safely. She also rented a room in a shared house to save money and avoid being tied to a long-term contract.

- **Willingness to Learn** – Matilde learned that language nuances are difficult to decipher.

6. ON A JOURNEY DOING THE BEST YOU CAN: NICOLE'S LIVING ABROAD STORY

One minute Nicole was in Canada, the next she was in Belgium starting a new life with her partner, Jeroen, whom she'd met just eight months earlier during a trip to the UK. "Where am I going and what am I thinking?" she'd said to a friend who had handed her a document titled 'Belgium – key facts' prior to boarding her flight. At the time of writing, Nicole has lived in Belgium for over twenty years. She speaks two languages.

Nicole **SINKS**

Culture shock
The wonderful yet brutally honest communication style in northern Belgium got to Nicole and still does. The same goes for spatial awareness. She regularly mutters sarcastically to herself, "Please don't step right in front of me when I'm reaching into the supermarket fridge," *and* "I don't recall asking for your opinion, but please do share."

Family and friends in shock
Nicole's decision to emigrate shocked her family and friends. Their reactions ranged from anger ("How could you do this?") to being thrilled ("Wow, this is an amazing adventure"). Many in the angry camp fell from Nicole's radar. She lost contact with them. The Volatility surrounding losing some people in her life was unsettling.

Language
Some shop assistants refused to speak English, pointing instead at words in a dictionary. Nicole's anxiety boiled over. Jeroen's family members were similarly intolerant, asking, "You've been here six months. When will you start language classes?" The pressure was intense, but the more pressure Nicole felt, the more she revolted. She subsequently put learning the language second to getting to grips with the new ways of doing things – which was more than enough to handle.

Where's Nicole?
"What's happened to me? Why can't I do this?" Nicole had been a successful business woman in Canada yet in Belgium she had become a fragment of her former self – she felt like a two-year-old. The enormity of her decision to emigrate was sinking in. She had been naïve about living abroad. Life abroad is Complex and creates Ambiguity. She began to dislike Belgium and the people. "They look like me but they're different," she said.

... and then SWIMS

Language
The relationship with her in-laws improved once she began learning the language. When she visits friends and family in Canada, however, her sentences become a mix of English and Flemish. Translating words in your head can result in confusion when you speak. But one thing is certain. "English is a part of my identity," she said. "It's my mother tongue, my emotional language."

Network
Nicole joined international communities and did some volunteer work to help with the integration challenges. "The connections I've made with others who were and remain in the same boat as me are deep," she said. She described the friendships she has developed as incredible – like a sisterhood. Her husband jokingly says that if they had a party, there would be someone from almost every country in the world.

Old age
Nicole feels uneasy at the thought of growing old and dying in Belgium. The sisterhood has a plan, however. They intend to live together, looking after one another in their old age.

Starting from scratch
After giving up her own business back home in Canada, Nicole decided to quash the Uncertainties she was feeling by reinventing herself in Belgium. She connected with others within her profession. This, along with networking, made all the difference. Her new business grew rapidly, taking on a life of its own.

> "This is my life script. I wouldn't change anything. I'm doing the best I can on my journey."
> **Nicole in Belgium**

Nicole's Living Abroad Learnings

Nicole's story highlights how living abroad brings Volatility, Uncertainty, Complexity and Ambiguity to the fore. Her experiences highlight how important it is to:

- Research the host country before emigrating.
- Realise that culture shock is real. Some cultural norms and behaviours may be challenging.
- Appreciate that family and friends may react differently to your decision to emigrate; some will be happy, while others won't be.
- Understand you may lose contact with some of your friends back home.
- Learn the language, although you may decide to place this second to getting to grips with the culture.
- Recognise that your native language is your emotional language.
- Join international networking groups.
- Do volunteer work.
- Consider what you will do in your old age if you remain in your host country long-term.
- Network and reach out to professionals in your line of work.

Nicole Got Leggy

Nicole viewed most of the challenges she faced as opportunities to push herself forward – to swim. Any negative, pessimistic and gloomy Thoughts and Emotions that arose were consequently quashed. When asked how she managed anger, fear and sadness, she said:

- **From Anger to Calm** – "I was shocked at how I was treated when I couldn't speak the language, but once I'd begun to come to terms with the different ways of doing things, I started language classes and began to feel less agitated."

- **From Fear to Confidence** – "I had no clue who I was anymore, and this frightened me. However, I found networking restored my identity."

- **From Sadness to Happiness** – "Losing some of my friends back home was hard, but I have since established a strong community of friends."

Nicole's Values and Strengths

Nicole's story highlights the Values and Strengths she draws on to manage her life abroad. They include:

- **Connections** – Nicole developed new friendships by joining networking groups and doing volunteer work. Through her connections, her new business grew.

- **Integrity** – Nicole was determined to remain true to being her authentic self and to hold on to her Canadian Values. She consequently gets annoyed when some of the Belgian ways clash with those in Canada.

- **Pragmatism** – Nicole placed learning the language second to getting to grips with Belgian culture. She also plans to live with her friends in old age.

7. PAY IT FORWARD: PAULINE'S LIVING ABROAD STORY

Pauline, originally from Spain, has lived abroad for a total of sixteen years. She speaks four languages. Her first move abroad was to Germany. When her work as an au pair ended, however, she repatriated. Years later, she fell in love with a Dutch guy while visiting her brother, who was studying in the Netherlands at the time. Done with her boring life in Spain, she emigrated for the second time.

Pauline **SINKS**

Behaviours
Spanish people care for one another *a lot*. When it's pouring with rain, cars give way so you and your children can safely cross the road. If you fall, there'll be fifty people coming to your assistance. In the Netherlands, it's different. After crashing into you on their bike, the Dutch carry on as if nothing happened. Pauline knows the Dutch can be kind and caring, but she seldom sees this in their behaviours. What's more, while the Spanish openly show their Emotions, the Dutch rarely do. Pauline wishes she had researched the Netherlands before relocating to find out more about the people and their culture. The Complexity and Ambiguity of Dutch culture was, in the beginning, all-consuming.

Home
Pauline rented a room in Amsterdam without a contract. When she returned from holiday, she was greeted by a family who had moved into her room. The landlord apologised but the trust between them was broken. Not knowing what to do or where to go, she turned to a trusted friend. The timing was perfect: he had a room to rent. Moving her belongings proved problematic, however. Credit cards were issued sparingly to the debt-averse Dutch. Pauline had subsequently not been able to secure one via her bank. Unable to pay for a hire car, she booked a taxi.

Limited friendships
It's been difficult for Pauline to make friends with the Dutch, many of whom have an already well-established circle of friends *and* busy calendars. Arranging an appointment for a chat and a coffee can take weeks, if not months. Pauline has a few Dutch friends who have lived abroad and know exactly what it feels like to not belong. "Locals don't understand how challenging integrating can be if they've never lived abroad," she said.

... and then SWIMS

Be you
Life in a small Spanish village where everyone knows one another had been stifling. The Netherlands was different and turned into a perfect opportunity to start afresh. "I love that I'm hardly known here," Pauline said. The Dutch were having difficulty pronouncing her name. She changed it to Polina. Adjusting to her new life, she began to feel more comfortable in her own skin. She's now the funny, emotionally expressive Spanish girl.

Language opens doors
When she first arrived in the Netherlands, Pauline had enough money to live on for a month. Within days, she'd secured a job as a waitress. It was a start but she didn't want this to be her forever job, even though she loved the work. After learning Dutch and improving her English, she secured a customer service role with an international company. Her career has since blossomed.

Networking
Pauline was welcomed in the Netherlands by several Israelis. These work colleagues became her away-from-home family, and even though her network has since expanded tenfold in this multi-cultural society, she and her Israeli friends remain close. She now supports newly-arrived internationals who are in the same situation she was in years ago. "Welcoming newcomers is my way of paying it forward for the help I received when I arrived in the Netherlands. It makes me feel good," she said.

Schools
Pauline is delighted her kids go to a Dutch rather than a Spanish school. In Dutch schools they work and play in groups from an early age, developing teamworking skills and behavioural traits such as calmness and confidence. What's more, in this structured teaching environment, children are taught to be mindful and respectful of each other.

> "Moving abroad is a great way to unleash the real you."
> **Pauline in the Netherlands**

Pauline's Living Abroad Learnings

Pauline's story highlights how living abroad brings Volatility, Uncertainty, Complexity and Ambiguity to the fore. Her experiences highlight how important it is to:

- Have a rental contract.
- Understand that credit card usage may be restricted in some countries.
- Identify how you will move home without your own transport.
- Research the host country before relocating.
- Realise that the behaviours of locals may be upsetting.
- Recognise that connecting with the locals may be difficult.
- Appreciate that locals may not be able to relate to the challenges of integrating.
- View living abroad as an opportunity to become your true self.
- Be flexible and open-minded about employment opportunities.
- Learn the language.
- Improve your English language skills.
- Recognise that your network may comprise almost solely of internationals.
- Assist other foreigners with their integration.
- Realise that the school system may be different.

Pauline Got Leggy

Pauline viewed most of the challenges she faced as opportunities to push herself forward – to swim. Any negative, pessimistic and gloomy Thoughts and Emotions that arose were consequently quashed. When asked how she managed anger, fear and sadness, she said:

- **From Anger to Calm** – "While I have a few Dutch friends, making friends with the Dutch has been frustrating. I have instead focused on developing friendships with other internationals."

- **From Fear to Confidence** – "I was anxious when I discovered my room had been re-let. Thankfully, a friend had a room I could rent. I was relieved that I could move on in more ways than one."

- **From Sadness to Happiness** – "I felt like I was suffocating in Spain, but in the Netherlands, I feel at peace. I've become the real me."

Pauline's Values and Strengths

Pauline's story highlights the Values and Strengths she draws on to manage her life abroad. They include:

- **Adaptability** – Moving to the Netherlands gave Pauline the opportunity to start afresh. She changed her name and became her true, authentic self – the funny, emotionally expressive Spanish girl.

- **Perseverance** – Pauline discovered that making friends with the Dutch was difficult. She consequently developed friendships with other internationals, some of whom she now supports on their integration journey.

- **Resilience** – Pauline instinctively knew she had to find another place to live when her landlord re-let her room. After learning Dutch and improving her English language skills, she secured a job in customer service.

🏊 SWIMMING LESSON EIGHT
Living Abroad

In Swimming Lesson Eight, you are asked to reflect on the stories you have read in this chapter and to identify ways in which you can adapt further to your host country.

Revisit the learnings in each living abroad story and list below what else you can do to adapt to your host country. For example:

I'll take classes to further develop my language skills.

I'll become a volunteer.

Chapter Summary

In this chapter you learned ...

Cultural Awareness

- Observe and copy the behaviours of locals to learn about and adapt to your host country's culture.
- Seek the reasons behind why things are different in your host country.
- Interpret culture norms.
- Locals don't always appreciate that things are done differently beyond their own country's borders.
- You may find that things in your home country are not readily available in your host country.
- Food may not be to your liking.
- You are the outsider. You, not the locals, need to adapt.
- The way things worked back home won't necessarily be the same in your host country.
- Become a tourist in your host country.

Language

- Learn the language.
- Languages may look the same but words may be pronounced differently and have different meanings.
- Identify where the emphasis is placed in both written and spoken language.
- Recognise that interpreting language nuances can be difficult.
- Appreciate that your native language is your emotional language.
- Understand that you may use a second language more than your native one.
- Realise natives may switch to English when they hear your accent.
- Acknowledge that English is not a global language.

Practicalities

- Research your host country before you depart.
- Make copies of official documents before you leave your home country.

- Organise a power of attorney in your home country.
- Recognise that you will need to start from the beginning in many aspects of your life.
- Establish existing routines on arrival.
- Realise there may be no-go areas where you live.
- Have a do-it-yourself mentality.
- Seek support and assistance.
- Have a rental contract in place.
- Consider sharing a house.
- Understand that credit card usage may be limited.
- School systems may be different.
- Consider and implement a plan for your old age if you intend to stay in your host country long-term.

Relationships

- Acknowledge that the relationship with your family and friends back home will change.
- Talk to strangers to learn about your host country and to establish new friendships.
- Develop relationships with both locals and internationals, knowing they may become your support network and even your friends.
- Join networking groups and hobby organisations.
- Avoid internationals who are critical of your host country.
- Family and friends may react differently to your decision to emigrate.
- Keep in contact with friends wherever you and they are in the world.
- Do volunteer work.
- Reach out to professionals in your field of work.
- Locals may not appreciate the challenges of integrating.
- Assist other foreigners on their integration journey.

Work

- Be flexible with your thinking about employment opportunities.
- Understand you may not be able to secure employment that's of equal status to what you had in your home country.
- Your qualifications and work experience may be valued less.
- You may need to study to gain new qualifications.

Self-Awareness

- Remain focused on the reason(s) for relocating.
- View living abroad as an opportunity to start afresh.
- Comprehend the importance of remaining true to your authentic self.
- Smile and laugh at the unusual and cultural quirks.
- Be aware that some cultures may not be right for you.
- Your Values and Strengths enable you to handle the challenges and opportunities of living abroad.
- Expect to first sink and then swim when you live abroad.

In this chapter you have completed one Swimming Lesson.

Congratulate yourself. You've earned your fifth swimming medal.

Useful Resources

- Read *Networking for People Who Hate Networking*. Devora Zack. 2019. Berrett-Koehler Publishers.
- Read *The Mobile Life*. Diane Lemieux & Anne Parker. 2013. XPat Media.
- Read *The Power of Strangers*. Joe Keohane. 2021. Penguin Books.
- Read *Transitions*. William Bridges. 2019. Lifelong Books.
- Read 'You lost me at Hello'. Patti McCarthy. https://www.linkedin.com/pulse/you-lost-me-hello-patti-mccarthy-nee-hewstone-/
- Watch *Hofstede Cultural Framework. Business School 101*. https://www.youtube.com/watch?v=TX0fUAhBAfc&t=60s

A Ripple of Laughter

I'm not so good at geography, but I know the name of one city in France. That's Nice.

CHAPTER SIX

Preparing for the Worst: Death of a Relative

*"Life is a series of hellos and goodbyes;
I'm afraid it's time for goodbye again."*

Billy Joel
American singer, songwriter and pianist

No Weddings, Just Funerals

- "I never got to say goodbye."
- "I won't ever see him again."
- "I wish I had …"

The death of a relative can be devastating, and never more so than when you live abroad. You wish you'd called more and you wish you'd had more time together, but now it's too late.

You're all at sea, swirling in Volatility, Uncertainty, Complexity and Ambiguity. You don't know what to do or who to turn to, and waves of fear, anger, confusion, loneliness and sadness wash over you. As the reality of the situation sinks in, you may realise that:

- Your family aren't reaching out to you – because you're not physically with them.
- Living thousands of kilometres away makes things complicated. Taking care of the deceased's affairs and attending the funeral is difficult.
    - Can you take time off – bereavement leave or a holiday?
    - Should your children go with you?
    - Can you afford to travel?

- The passing hasn't changed how you feel about the fractured and perhaps even estranged relationships with family members.
- You don't know your deceased relative's wishes and they're no longer around to ask.
- There's no will.
- You are the executor of the will yet no longer know how things work back home. You are no longer a resident, and processing the paperwork isn't going to be easy.

We plan diligently for weddings. From the guest list to rings, everything for the big day is scrupulously taken care of. When it comes to death, however, there is often no plan.

Linda Bellingham, a British actress most notably known for her role in the James Herriot *All Creatures Great and Small* television series, died of cancer in 2014. Immediately following her diagnosis, she began planning for her death. In her book *There's Something I've Been Dying to Tell You*, she shared the importance of being open with family members, even when there is a reluctance to speak. For some, however, death is a taboo subject, a difficult, if not impossible, subject. Nevertheless, it is an inevitable part of life. Discussing a relative's wishes before they die is an absolute must.

When you relocated abroad, you likely gave little to no thought to a relative dying. I know I didn't. However, during the twenty-two years I have lived abroad, six family members have passed. I have dealt with funeral arrangements, been the executor of wills and administered estates. Preparing for the worst by understanding your relatives' wishes and what to do when they pass is crucial – and more so when you live abroad.

In the stories that follow, Anna and Pauline share how they dealt with the death of one or more relatives while living abroad.

Calling to Say Goodbye
Anna's Story – Death of a Relative

In *Chapter Five* we met Anna, who has lived abroad almost all her life. Originally from Spain she is, at the time of writing, living in Sweden. Her Values and Strengths of connections, pragmatism and resilience not only came to the fore in her living abroad story but are once again highlighted here – in her account of how she dealt with the death of her cousin Abigail.

Cousins and Big Sisters

Anna and Abigail, both only children, lived together from a young age. Anna's mother had helped raise her niece from being a baby. "We were more than just cousins, more like big sisters," Anna said. In adulthood, they remained close despite the physical distance between them.

Anna, to put it mildly, was shocked when she learned of Abigail's cancer diagnosis. Her big sister was going to die before her time. "Death comes to us all, but we shouldn't have to say goodbye to the young," said Anna.

Desperate to spend as much time as possible with her big sister, Anna flew to the States twice a year. In 2020, however, these visits were abruptly halted; the Covid-19 Pandemic travel restrictions made sure of that. Anna was distraught. How could she support her big sister so far away? Calling her regularly and writing to her was the best she could do. When they spoke, they talked about anything and everything but the big C. Abigail hadn't wanted to talk about her illness.

Calling and Coping

Abigail died in March 2021.

Anna spoke with her cousin three days before she passed, unaware of how ill she was. The night before she died, Abigail's husband called. Abigail was in and out of consciousness and was slipping away. Unsure if her big sister could hear her or understand what she was saying, Anna told Abigail how she felt about her. She sincerely hoped her words had been comforting. The call had been difficult beyond belief, and putting the phone down even more so. "At least I'd had the opportunity to say goodbye, but I hadn't wanted her to pass," she said with tears in her eyes. Not being able to see Abigail had been heartbreaking. Sadness and anger consumed her.

On the day of Abigail's funeral, Anna took the day off work. Through the kitchen window she noticed frost glistening on the grass. It was spring and temperatures were rising. *I'll sit outside later*, she said to herself.

Later that day, not wanting to spill a drop of her hot chocolate, Anna walked gingerly to the bench at the corner of the terrace. Nestling herself into her favourite rainbow-coloured cushion, she stared at the daffodils dancing in the breeze. The frost was melting now. Droplets trickled over the bright yellow petals. At that very moment, Abigail's funeral was taking place thousands of miles away. Anna took a slurp of her hot chocolate. Tears began to flow, warm tears in a cool breeze.

Getting Leggy

"I didn't cope at all well. I was overwhelmed, wallowing in grief," Anna confessed. She wished she had sought emotional support from her parents, but she hadn't wanted to add to their burden. They, too, were grieving.

Anna carefully handpicked who she could process her Thoughts and Emotions with, having recognised that people don't talk openly in such situations. Her aunt was one of the people she spoke to. Abigail's daughter, Carol, was another. Reaching out and talking about Abigail helped them all cope with their loss.

In her diary, Anna documented precious memories she had of her and Abigail. Doing so was comforting. Her main support, however, came from her husband and their two children. She felt safe within the four walls of her home. It was where she could let go, let her Emotions flow. She later underwent therapy to manage her grief and to release lingering, pent-up Emotions.

Therapy on Your Doorstep

Not long after Abigail's funeral, Anna took some time off. She didn't want to venture far, nor did she need to. Living in Sweden, a country crammed with lakes and dense forests, was perfect. North of Stockholm, she enjoyed the peace and quiet of the deep, dark blue Riddarfjärden and the seemingly endless Romme Alpin Forest. Having recently learned to row, she took to the water. "When I'm in the boat I don't think about work or other things. I let my mind drift, focusing only on how I'm going to get to where I want to go," she said. When she took in the beauty of her surroundings, flashbacks of her and Abigail as children in a rowing boat with her parents began to surface. This was the best therapy ever. Anna was calm, and a sense of happiness enveloped her. Moving forward in her life without Abigail wasn't going to be easy, but with countless memories to draw on, she'd manage.

Closure

A year after Abigail's death, a memorial service was arranged. Once again, Anna was unable to attend, this time due to work commitments. Desperate to be a part of the service in some shape or form, she reached out to Abigail's friends and to Abigail's end-of-life nurse.

"Can I contribute?" she asked them. "Can I watch online?"

But none of that was possible. The service was to be casual. Wanting to contribute in some way, Anna found photos of her and Abigail as children for the memorial wall.

On the evening before the service, Anna went to an Elton John concert. Dancing and singing to one of Abigail's favourite artists was uplifting. "Listening to music helps me recall memories of Abigail. Along with photos I have of her around my home, this brings me joy in all the sadness," she said, smiling. Anna regularly listens to a playlist of hits – hits she and Abigail used to listen to.

"When it's not possible to be present to say goodbye to loved ones, you question whether they've actually gone," Anna said. She intends to meet her big sister's colleagues when she next travels to the USA. Hearing their stories, learning more about Abigail, will be a great opportunity to gain closure. She also feels it will assist her with her lingering grief. Closure is a lot harder when you live abroad.

Anna continues to do things that keep Abigail alive in her life.

The Next Goodbye

Losing Abigail brought home the reality of the next goodbyes – Anna's parents. They live in the USA, and the distance is challenging. She would like them to move to Sweden but for now that's not happening.

Since Abigail's passing, Anna has spoken with her parents about their wishes. Knowing whether they want to be buried or cremated and whether they want a religious service or not has relieved some of the burden she will face at the time of their passing. She has also spoken with her husband about his parents' wishes – and about their own. What's the first thing you do when someone passes? Should we take out funeral insurance? What about inheritance and how does this work across borders? What about selling the home and what about the house contents? Who are the utility providers? What are the codes and passwords to things? The list is endless. "These conversations are not pleasant but they are necessary," said Anna. The details help remove the burden and Uncertainties when a relative passes.

Living abroad added layers of difficulty to the passing of Anna's big sister. The Volatility, Complexity and Ambiguity arising from not being able to see Abigail before she passed or attend her funeral or memorial service was beyond distressing. All Anna could do was contribute as best she could from the sidelines.

"For forty-nine years Abigail had been a big part of my life. I miss her dearly."

> "Do something that brings you joy in all the sadness."
> **Anna in Sweden**

Champagne and Bracelets
Pauline's Story – Death of Two Relatives

In *Chapter Five* we met Pauline. She's the one who emigrated to the Netherlands for love and to escape a boring life in her homeland, Spain. Her Values and Strengths of adaptability, perseverance and resilience highlighted in her living abroad story come to the fore once again here – in her account of how she dealt with the deaths of her mum and dad just eight months apart.

Difficult Relationships

Pauline's parents had been separated for almost fifteen years. Her dad, Antonio, who was retired, lived an isolated life. While he loved to see Pauline, her husband, Niek, and his grandchildren, he only ever wanted to do so for short periods. "We can have breakfast together. We don't need to see each other more than that," he'd say. Pauline's relationship with her mum, Isabel, also retired, was strained. On occasion, Isabel had made it clear she felt a closer bond with Pauline's brother, Javier.

Pauline's relationship with her parents was riddled with Volatility and Complexity, and the physical distance between them only exacerbated the emotional distance she felt. Nevertheless, she called them regularly and visited as often as she could.

Deteriorating Health

In late 2022, Antonio had a spate of falls, but numerous medical examinations found nothing. Pauline booked a flight to Spain, realising her dad's health was deteriorating and believing it could be the last time she would see him.

The following day, her dad called. Now it was Isabel who was in hospital. A blockage of a vein leading to her heart had been discovered.

"I'm worried about your mum's lifestyle," he said.

Isabel was a heavy smoker, but who was *he* to talk about lifestyle? He wasn't exactly in a good place himself. His home and health were a mess.

Her dad began swearing. "If you agree with me, fine. If not, f*ck you."

Pauline knew her dad could be emotionally Volatile, but how he was now speaking to her was unacceptable. She hung up.

Minutes later he called back. "You're young, you're never here, and you have no idea what your mum gets up to." Clearly, his rant wasn't over.

Pauline had expected an apology, but that wasn't happening. When the call ended, she rang her brother. "I'm cancelling my flight. I'm not coming."

Getting Leggy

Within minutes of cancelling her flight, the simmering anger Pauline had felt fizzled away. She had put a boundary in place with her dad, and it felt liberating. However, she now needed time to unravel her Thoughts and Emotions. Turning to Niek and her best friend for support, sadness enveloped her. Her tears flowed. She knew deep down that she ought to be in Spain supporting her parents, but deep-rooted, raw emotional pain had surfaced. Maybe her dad had lashed out because he realised his own health and lifestyle weren't good? Reasoning with and Getting Leggy with her Thoughts and Emotions brought relief. Pauline felt calm.

Not a Cent Over

Pauline called her brother the following morning. Javier, who was with their dad at the time, handed the phone to Antonio.

"I'm sorry," Antonio said. "I don't know what happened yesterday."

Pauline accepted his apology but chose not to discuss the situation further.

The following day she asked her manager if she could work from Spain for three months. Pauline and Niek drove to Spain with their children and their dog.

Antonio was bed-bound at home and had open wounds that weren't healing. What she saw was beyond shocking, and adding to that shock was the state of her dad's finances. He needed a new mattress but had no money: every cent of his pension was being absorbed to pay for scams he'd fallen for. Pauline and Niek had enough money to pay for incontinence pads and a few hours of care, but after paying childcare fees and renting an apartment, there was nothing left. She felt helpless.

Adding to her helplessness were the Covid-19 Pandemic restrictions, which prevented her from visiting her mum in hospital. Pauline's priority was now her dad, who was seriously ill. That was until her mum was discharged from hospital after having been informed there was nothing that could be done. Pauline, Niek and their children visited Isabel as often as they could.

Champagne Ending

After three months of caring for her parents, it was time for her son to go back to school and for her and Niek to go back to the office. Antonio understood.

"Your life isn't here. Go home. I'll be fine," he said.

But the next day, Pauline received a call from the carer. "I don't know what's happening, but your dad's speech is slurred," she said.

"Call 112," Pauline replied, suspecting her dad was having a stroke. Her hunch was right, and Pauline remained in Spain on her own.

"Get me a bottle of champagne," her dad mumbled, barely coherent, when Pauline visited him in hospital the next day. Pauline sensed what her father was thinking – *I'm going to die soon, so let me do so in style.*

Pauline visited her dad every day. He listened and smiled as she shared stories of her life in the Netherlands. On February 23rd 2023, he passed.

Isabel dealt with the funeral arrangements, and afterwards, Pauline was at last able to go home to her family.

Identical Bracelets

Isabel, Pauline and Javier decided to engage a solicitor to work through Antonio's extremely messy financial affairs and to sell his assets.

In September 2023, Pauline returned to Spain to finalise her father's estate. She and her mum spent one evening remembering Antonio and reflecting on their own lives while watching the moon rise over a stormy Balearic sea.

"This is the best feeling ever," Isabel said, turning to her daughter. "I'm sorry for some of the things I've said," she continued. "I *do* love you." Their tears flowed.

The following day, Pauline handed her mum a bracelet. "What's this for?" she asked as Pauline placed a second, identical bracelet on her own wrist. But her daughter had no words. As they hugged, they sensed a new connection forming between them.

Pauline called her mum regularly after returning to the Netherlands.

Signs

One morning, Pauline's daughter said to her, "*Abuela* [Grandma] is in heaven." Pauline smiled. "No, sweetheart. *Abuelo* [Grandpa] is in heaven, not *Abuela*."

Two weeks later, while Pauline took a walk in Amsterdam woods, she reflected on what her daughter had said. Shivers ran down her spine. She spoke briefly with her mum later that day.

That night, Pauline woke suddenly. It was five minutes past midnight. Three missed calls from an unknown Spanish number displayed on her phone. Shaking, Pauline called the number.

"It's your mum," said an old family friend. "I'm so sorry."

Sobbing, Pauline dropped to her knees.

Within minutes, a text arrived from Javier. "Mom's passed away. Call me."

Pauline was on the first flight out of Amsterdam later that morning. It was October 17th 2023. Just eight months after her dad had passed.

Commiserations

As Pauline and Javier confirmed the body they were staring at was their mum's, disbelief consumed them. An hour later, they collected Isabel's dog from the animal protection home. Making noises they had never heard before, he too was grieving. When they opened the door to Isabel's apartment, the trauma continued. There was an ashtray full of cigarette stubs next to an oxygen inhaler. It said it all. Feeling their mother's presence, the siblings sobbed in each other's arms.

Arranging the funeral was next on their long to-do list, but they had no idea what their mum's wishes had been. They knew she had liked Antonio's coffin and that she loved blue eyeliner and red lipstick. The rest, however, was guesswork. Isabel's many friends attended the funeral to say their goodbyes.

A few weeks later, there was a call from the solicitor who had dealt with Antonio's estate and who was now dealing with Isabel's. Some unexpected family insurance had arrived. It covered the funeral costs.

Days later, Pauline and Javier went to their mum's favourite beach to scatter her ashes. It was a beautiful moment, one forever imprinted in their minds. The loss of both their parents in such a short period of time had been devastating. Now it was just the two of them.

Gratitude

Compared to some of her friends who have parents with long-term illnesses, Pauline feels grateful. Her dad had died after a short illness and her mum from a heart attack just eight months later. Her gratitude extends to her husband, children and best friend, all of whom kept her sane and afloat for an arduous eighteen months. It had been a Volatile, Uncertain, Complex and Ambiguous period in her life, one she will never forget.

> "We all have difficult family relationships and difficult situations to deal with. How we cope when the two combine is up to us."
> **Pauline in the Netherlands**

Anna and Pauline's Tips – Death of a Relative

When preparing for and managing the death of a relative, Anna and Pauline stressed how important it is to:

Finances

- Check if there is funeral insurance.
- Recognise that travelling to your relative's country can be costly and more so if you need to stay there for a period of time.
- Appreciate there may be no money to cover a dying relative's care needs.

Health

- Express how you are feeling with people you trust.
- Write a diary. Include memories of the deceased.
- Go outside into nature.
- Take time out to reflect on your loss.
- Do something you enjoy, for example, rowing or walking in the woods.
- Recall memories:
  - Share stories with your dying relative.
  - Listen to music and look at photos of the deceased.

- Work with a therapist or counsellor to assist with your grief and to release Emotions.
- Recognise that family conflicts and tensions can bubble over prior to a relative dying.
- Put boundaries in place when Emotions run high.

Legal

- Write your own will.
- Engage a solicitor to manage the estate administration.
- Investigate inheritance laws in your home and host country to understand your rights.

Other

- Document *everything* related to your relative's daily life, including but not limited to details of energy suppliers, pensions, bank account numbers, house alarm codes and passwords.
- Appreciate the practicalities involved when someone dies, including identifying the body, attending to pets, arranging the funeral, dealing with finances and disposing of assets.

Relationships

- Speak with relatives about their funeral wishes, for example, burial or cremation.
- Communicate with your relative if you know they are dying.
  - Write and call regularly.
  - Visit them before they die where possible.
- Respect your relative's wishes. Talk about something else if they don't want to speak about their illness.
- Take time off if you are unable to attend the funeral.
- Attend the funeral online, if possible.
- Communicate with people the deceased person knew.
- Talk with and seek support from family and friends.

Work

- Ask to work abroad while caring for a dying relative.

🏊 SWIMMING LESSON NINE
Death of a Relative

In Swimming Lesson Nine, you are asked to reflect on the death stories in this chapter.

List below the actions you intend to take to prepare for the death of a relative while living abroad. Set a deadline against each action. For example:

Speak with Mum about her funeral wishes – March 2025.

Chapter Summary

Preparing for the Worst – Death of a Relative
Sue's Final Comments

When you receive news of the passing of a relative, you may feel like you are sinking. However, as you wade through the numerous questions and practicalities requiring your attention, you realise you have a wealth of resources to draw on. These include:

- Learnings from your integration journey.
- Getting Leggy with any negative, pessimistic and gloomy Thoughts and Emotions.
- The living abroad tips shared in *Chapter Five*.
- The death of a relative tips shared by Anna and Pauline in this chapter.
- Your own proposed actions on how to deal with the death of a relative detailed in *Swimming Lesson Nine*.

You can manage this, knowing that first you sink and then you swim.

In this chapter you learned …

- How to prepare for the worst – the death of a relative when living abroad.
- The importance of being open, honest and proactive with relatives concerning the subject of death, including:
  - Documenting the wishes of family members.
  - Writing a plan to reduce and hopefully eliminate any Uncertainties that arise when a relative dies.
  - Encouraging relatives to write a will.
- To communicate regularly with a relative who is dying.
- To visit a dying relative where possible.
- There are countless things to do, from funeral arrangements to estate administration.
- When you hear news of the passing of a relative, decide if you can attend the funeral, and find ways to look after yourself.
- To seek professional, emotional, psychological and legal help as necessary.

In this chapter you have completed one Swimming Lesson.

Congratulate yourself. You've earned your sixth swimming medal.

Useful Resources

- Read 'Death happens – plan for it'. www.moneysavingexpert.com/family/death-plan
- Read *On Grief and Grieving*. Elisabeth Kübler-Ross and David Kessler. 2014. Simon & Schuster Inc.
- Read *With the End in Mind*. Kathryn Mannix. 2017. William Collins.
- Watch *Clowning around: A show that tackles death and grief*. BBC. https://www.bbc.com/news/av/stories-51327721
- Watch *Dealing with Death Whilst Living Abroad*. JaDan. https://www.youtube.com/watch?v=QyEjJiLv_A4

A Ripple of Laughter

Why is there a fence around the cemetery?
Because people are dying to get in.

Source: https://explainthejoke.com/2023/02/19/the-graveyards-edge

CHAPTER SEVEN

Storms Don't Last Forever: Divorce and Separation

"If you are going through hell, keep going."
Winston Churchill
Prime Minister of the United Kingdom in office during the Second World War

Has Our Ship Sailed?

- "Our marriage is over. I want a divorce."
- "I've had enough. I need a break."
- "I don't fit in here. I'm moving back home."

Whether it's your decision to divorce or separate or your partner's, the foundation on which your life abroad exists is shaken to the core. Whether you saw the situation coming or not, instigated the situation or not, every aspect of your life can be affected – your relationships, your children, your finances, your work and, last but not least, your health.

If you're the one delivering the news, you're adamant that your and your partner's ship has sailed. Your Thoughts are entrenched: you need to move on as soon as possible.

If you're receiving the news, you hope your and your partner's ship hasn't sailed. You intend to do anything and everything to salvage your relationship.

You're all at sea, swirling in Volatility, Uncertainty, Complexity and Ambiguity. You don't know what to do or who to turn to, and waves of fear, anger, confusion, loneliness and sadness wash over you. As the reality of the situation sinks in, you want and need to know:

- Do you have the legal right to remain in your host country?
- Where will you live?
- Do you need a solicitor?
- Will you have to go to court and how long will the proceedings take?
- How much is this going to cost?
- Who will gain custody of your child(ren)?

Divorce rates are known to be higher for couples living abroad. In her article 'Till stress do us part: the causes and consequences of expatriate divorce', Yvonne McNulty identifies two reasons for why people divorce when living abroad:

1. You live abroad.
2. Absence of a strong support network.

These will likely come as no surprise. As we saw in *Chapter Five*, connecting with others and creating new friendships was a common challenge for all. What's more, some international assignments involve frequent business travel for one of the partners. The other partner is left home alone, sometimes with children, sometimes not, to establish a new life in an unfamiliar country. The weight on their shoulders can be too much to bear. Living apart abroad is not uncommon and is likely another reason for high divorce rates *and* separation.

When you relocated abroad you likely gave little to no thought to divorce or separation. I know I didn't, and while Hans and I have never divorced or separated, we have lived apart. In 2013 I repatriated to the UK having been unable to secure employment in Norway. The ensuing bi-weekly commute rocked the foundation of our relationship. When I returned to Norway a year later, we began picking up the pieces of our splintered marriage.

When I was three, my parents divorced. My mum re-married when I was seven, but this second marriage failed just four years later. Divorce and separation can be severe storms, amounting to the worst years of your life, but they don't last forever. Understanding what to do when divorce or separation impacts Your World is crucial – especially when you live abroad.

In the stories that follow, Nicole and Laura share their experiences of living abroad while dealing with divorce and separation, respectively.

Whirlwind Romances Are Awesome but Sometimes Shit Happens
Nicole's Story – Divorce

In *Chapter Five* we met Nicole, who, in 1999, emigrated to Belgium to live with her partner, Jeroen. Some of her treasured Canadian friends subsequently fell by the wayside, but she soon established a new circle of friends who became her lifeline when her marriage to Jeroen crumbled. Nicole's Values and Strengths of connections, integrity and pragmatism not only came to the fore in her living abroad story but are once again highlighted here – in her account of how she dealt with divorce.

Scepticism Runs Rife

Nicole's arrival in Belgium was a baptism of fire. Within two months she married Jeroen, and six weeks later her father died. This, on top of establishing herself in her new country, getting to know her new in-laws and building a new business from scratch, was tough.

Despite her busyness, it wasn't long before Nicole started to have doubts about her marriage. Something wasn't right. This was Jeroen's second marriage, and Nicole began to wonder if his divorce had had something to do with his behavioural traits. He blamed others for his problems and believed he knew everything. "No one talked to me about *me*," Jeroen would say, turning to Nicole after visiting friends. Attempting to get her husband to see things from a different perspective, she suggested he participate in their friends' conversations. She later confronted him about his first marriage, but his reply was far from reassuring. "If I'd told you, I don't think you'd have married me," he said. After that, their relationship continued on a different footing.

Nicole and Jeroen spent years in marriage guidance. But every time Nicole sensed they were moving forward, Jeroen would pull out of the sessions. Her mental health began to suffer. Believing her husband needed her help, and wanting a stable home life for their daughter, Sofia, she stuck with him.

After falling ill in 2009, Jeroen joined a self-help group. Unbeknown to Nicole, he was not only using their life savings to attend group courses but was also having a relationship with a woman in the group. "We're done.

There's nothing more to discuss," Nicole snapped after learning of his deceit and infidelity. No longer able to trust her husband, she filed for divorce.

Jeroen wanted an out-of-court settlement. Nicole refused. The acrimonious divorce was painful beyond belief.

One School Teacher and Three Solicitors

"Children, we have some bad news," Sofia's teacher said to the class. "The mummy and daddy of Sofia are divorcing. So can you be kind to her?"

Sofia ran home crying. Still sobbing, she asked her parents, "Are you getting divorced?"

The day before, Jeroen and Nicole had informed the teacher of their intention to divorce. They wanted her to be alert to any changes in their daughter's performance and behaviour and had specifically asked for the news to be kept quiet. Nicole was furious, and to this day Sofia recalls this incident as one of her earliest traumas in life.

"If my client cannot get a reasonable outcome to raise her child, she will go back to Canada," Nicole's solicitor said to the judge. The possibility of Nicole and Sofia leaving Belgium had never been discussed or even considered. To state this in court was totally irresponsible and unforgivable. The solicitor had made a huge mistake and he knew it. Nicole and Sofia were now a flight risk, and, as of that moment, the judge forbade them from leaving the country. Nicole's solicitor quit. Devastated, she hired a second solicitor. Three months later, however, this solicitor suffered a heart attack. Solicitor number three not only failed to do his due diligence, he also didn't fight Nicole's case.

The court's decision made for unpleasant reading. "I was granted half of the child maintenance allowance for my daughter," said Nicole. "That was it. Nothing more." Nicole kicked Jeroen out of the family home, wanting this chapter of her life closed.

The court had also ruled that Jeroen must see his daughter one day a week and every other weekend, but when Sofia stayed with him, she slept in the hallway. Raging, Nicole returned to court.

"It's not ideal but my apartment is small. I have no choice," Jeroen said to the judge, who subsequently instructed him to sleep in the living room. Sofia was to sleep in her dad's bedroom.

"You see, these things can be taken care of easily," the judge said, looking directly at Nicole.

While the judge had agreed with her, he was dismissive of what he deemed to be a minor situation, one that could have been resolved out of court. Nicole was both alarmed and dismayed by his lack of empathy and compassion.

Where Are the Divorce Papers?

Six months after the court ruling, Nicole, who was still waiting to sign the divorce papers, received a letter out of the blue. The papers would not be signed off until she paid Jeroen's debt, a debt amounting to almost seventy thousand euros. "That letter brought me to my knees. I had no idea how I would ever get through this," she said. Up to this point she'd been managing the nightmare situation single-handedly. But now it was too much to bear. Getting Leggy with her anger and loneliness, she reached out to her network of friends for support and advice. Her news spread like wildfire.

"We need to talk. I'm coming over," the husband of a close friend said. Outraged by Jeroen's behaviour, he told Nicole they were going to help her counter-sue Jeroen. He and his wife would pay the legal fees.

Nicole's fourth solicitor was feisty. "What happened with Nicole's previous solicitors is not going to happen on my watch," she said during a meeting with Jeroen, Jeroen's solicitor and Nicole. After revealing they were aware of Jeroen's extramarital affairs, she declared that Nicole would not pay for any of his debts. "This case is going back to court."

Jeroen and his solicitor left the room in shock and disbelief. When they returned soon afterwards, Jeroen's solicitor sheepishly informed Nicole she didn't have to pay for anything. "We're done," he said. And after almost fifteen years of marriage, their divorce was finally settled.

Small Rewards

Walking home, Nicole decided to treat herself. *A cup of cappuccino won't break my already almost non-existent bank balance*, she thought. She sat under a patio heater and gazed down the street towards Antwerp's Central Station. Daylight was fading but the station's beautiful Gothic architecture was sparkling with bright white Christmas lights. Nicole had forgotten what it was like to take in the beauty of her home city, having for so long been engrossed in the divorce proceedings. Her broken Thoughts created a vivid picture of the evening ahead, a cosy evening in with her daughter. *Sofa, Sofia, girlie movies. What the hell. Let's add a box of those delicious Belgian chocolates to our cosy evening in. We've earned this.* It was now time for Nicole and Sofia to get on with their lives. Well, almost …

Health Matters

When Sofia turned eighteen, she was no longer legally obliged to see her dad. She stopped visiting him immediately, and the trauma therapy sessions she had been attending regularly to help cope with these visits and her parents' divorce also stopped.

Nicole's health had also suffered. After throwing herself into her work, burnouts became a recurring theme, and once the divorce was finalised, she contracted a superbug. "I was experiencing complete implosion," said Nicole.

Giving and Receiving

Nicole felt she had experienced the ultimate in suffering. But while she was incensed by the unfairness of what had happened, she was also greatly appreciative of the support she and Sofia had received from her friends. One friend bought her a book suggesting she might write what she was grateful for every day. *My pen works* was her first entry. "Even in the worst moments there is always something to be grateful for," she said.

Other friends rallied round during her darkest hours. Bags of clothes appeared on the doorstep, cash was left in the letterbox, and the most spectacular of birthday parties were organised for Sofia.

"I have no idea how I will repay you," Nicole told her friends. Their reply was always the same. Nicole owed them nothing. "That love you opened up in me to help you, changed me," one of her friends had told her.

Nicole now runs a support group, a group for women who, following divorce, separation or loss of their partner, have been left with nothing. It's her way of giving back and showing appreciation to her friends for their support.

Reflections

Reflecting on her relationship with Jeroen and their divorce, Nicole quoted Charles Dickens' *A Tale of Two Cities*. "It was the best of times, it was the worst of times."

The whirlwind romance with Jeroen had been just that. Unprepared for what followed, she was battered from all angles by Volatility, Uncertainty, Complexity and Ambiguity. The journey of living abroad and living in an unstable relationship that ultimately led to divorce had been ugly.

Nicole wishes she'd had a different relationship with Jeroen and that Sofia could have had a good relationship with her dad. She is acutely aware, however, that had their relationship been different, she would not have been blessed with wonderful friends. "I love my daughter *and* my friends and have created a beautiful, rich tapestry in my life," she said.

> "Matters of the heart are wonderful, but don't let your heart rule your head. Be prepared for a lot of misery if you don't do your due diligence."
> **Nicole in Belgium**

Third Time Lucky?
Laura's Story – Separation

In *Chapter Five* we met Laura, who described her life abroad as like living on parallel tracks. On one track, she did her utmost to remain true to who she is, her authentic self, while on the other, she attempted to adjust to her host country's culture. Laura's Values and Strengths of connections, humour and integrity highlighted in her living abroad story come to the fore again here – in her account of her separation from her partner.

Long-Distance Relationship

Laura and Olav met while studying in England for their master's degrees. It was 2004. After graduating, they returned to their respective homelands, Croatia and Norway. A long-distance relationship had begun.

Laura moved to Norway to be with Olav in 2013, but when her three-month visitor visa expired, she returned to Croatia. A year later, having secured a job in Norway, she returned, but when her temporary employment contract expired, she once again returned to Croatia. Securing employment of a similar status to what she was used to in Croatia was proving to be impossible in Norway, and with financial independence of critical importance to her, she never wanted to be a kept woman.

Laura knew Olav would never emigrate to Croatia. The onus was always on her to move to Norway. However, short-term visas and temporary employment contracts were putting a boulder in the way of her realising a consistent income stream as well as building a stable face-to-face relationship with Olav. But in 2015 he convinced her it was time to put an end to their long-distance relationship. Their son Jakov, four at the time, had only ever lived with his mum and barely knew his father. It was time to live together as a family.

Shortly afterwards, Laura and Jakov's family reunion application was approved by the Norwegian authorities.

A Monster Child Protection Service

Five weeks after Laura relocated, an argument broke out between the two of them. They were disagreeing about which nursery Jakov should go to. Laura lost her temper. She wanted her son to go to the nursery near where she worked. Olav, on the other hand, wanted him to go to the one near home. Moving in with Olav, learning the language, starting a new job, and now Jakov starting nursery – it had all become too much. Olav was now having a say in matters concerning their son. The situation was eating her alive. She was becoming more and more negative and felt she was losing control. They'd had petty arguments in the past, but this one was by far the worst.

Viewing Laura's behaviour as detrimental to Jakov, Olav rang the child welfare authorities, accusing her of violence. Within twenty minutes two armed welfare officers arrived. It was just after midnight. Laura, gripped by fear, agreed with the officers' request to allow Jakov to spend the night with Olav's parents.

Early the following morning she rang the authorities. What she was told was beyond distressing. She could only speak with Olav via them or via a solicitor, and she would need a court order to see her son. "This was cruel and inhuman," said Laura. "All I wanted was to resolve the situation calmly and sensibly with Olav, but they were having none of it." Most of all, she wanted her son back.

Laura later discovered that had she refused the officers' request, Jakov could have remained with her. Taking her son from her had not been legally enforceable. Olav had known that. He'd known the child custody rules; Laura hadn't. She felt tricked and betrayed.

Reunited

Laura and Jakov had been separated for five weeks when she learned they were to be reunited. While thrilled and relieved, Uncertainty and Ambiguity remained over what would happen next. "I was imprisoned in a country I hardly knew and locked in a judicial system fighting for the custody of my son, custody I already had. There was nothing to explain. How had it come to this?" The circumstances were surreal and excruciatingly painful. Guilt and shame consumed Laura.

Having been ordered by the authorities to leave the family home, Olav was now living with his parents, and Jakov saw his father during weekends.

Not One but Two Solicitors

Fearing Olav would gain custody of Jakov, Laura hired both a Croatian and a Norwegian solicitor. She needed to fight to keep her son no matter the cost. The Croatian came recommended by her sister, herself a lawyer. Nevertheless, Laura was placing enormous trust in this lawyer. A positive outcome was the only possibility.

The case was Complex. With no partnership agreement in place, the two solicitors worked meticulously through the Croatian and Norwegian child custody laws. Concurrently, Laura and Olav attended countless interviews with social services. Every bit of information about their relationship was scrutinised. "Without the solicitors, I dread to think what the outcome would have been," said Laura. "I had a partner whose intention was to gain custody of Jakov, and I had come face-to-face with a monster child protection system. Keeping my son was non-negotiable."

Escapism

Laura was lonely. She kept a lot of what was happening to herself. Forbidden from leaving Norway until the child custody case concluded, she was drowning in a cocktail of Emotions brought on by the Volatility of the situation she was in. All she wanted was for her and her son to be back with family and friends in Croatia.

When Jakov was in nursery, Laura would sit on the sofa attempting to escape reality. Remembering the good times, she'd picture herself having a beer or two with friends in downtown Zagreb, listening and dancing to live music. Then she'd be buying fresh produce from Dolac farmers' market to make her and Jakov's favourite dish, Sataraš. And then the sound of the communal garage door opening directly under her apartment would interrupt her Thoughts and the memories would quickly fade from view. *Time for another coffee*, she'd tell herself. *Time to get on with some household chores.* These fleeting Thoughts and memories helped Laura, albeit briefly, to escape the nightmare she was living. And somehow, they helped her to forgive herself for everything that had happened. "I'd been naïve about emigrating to Norway and moving in with Olav," said Laura. Living one day to the next, she was existing, not living.

Getting Leggy

When Jakov was with his dad, Laura would venture into her local park, Oslo's famous Vigeland sculpture park, housing over two hundred sculptures of the human body. She loved the vibrance of the park whatever the weather but there was always one sculpture that got to her. It was Sinnataggen, the little boy famous for his determined posture and the angry look on his face. This cute statue was almost always surrounded by people giggling, smiling and taking photos. Laura would smile, too, and sometimes giggle. "He's a happy little boy," she'd say, thinking of Jakov.

On other days she'd go ice-skating or go to church. "I'm not in any way religious. Going to church was never a thing of mine, but it helped me *a lot*," she said. The new friends she made helped keep her hopes alive and calmed the fears she had of losing Jakov.

Laura Got Leggy with her loneliness, fear and sadness. She not only found joy walking in Oslo's sculpture park but by plucking up the courage to go to church, she also found a handful of supportive friends.

Fragile Relationship

Almost one year to the day that armed social services officers arrived at the family home, the courts ruled in Laura's favour. Jakov was Croatian, born out of wedlock. Laura, a foreigner, had no means of residing in Norway alone. By default, Laura had full custody of Jakov. Olav's intentions had indeed been to gain custody of his son, something he would never have been granted in Croatia. Olav agreed to the court ruling and signed the papers. The case was closed, and with it, the Volatility, Uncertainty, Complexity and Ambiguity that had enveloped Laura's life withered away. Laura and Jakov returned home to Croatia within days.

"Going to court was the only way to get my son back," Laura said. The child protection system had been harsh, failing to give her and her partner an opportunity to resolve the situation together. Reflecting on her experience, Laura admitted she should have been more careful. Moving to a country she barely knew had put her and her son in a vulnerable situation. "Out of wedlock relationships are fragile," said Laura. "There are no guarantees."

Jakov now visits his father during school holidays, and from time to time Laura and Olav see one another in their respective countries. The tide never turned in favour of Laura and Olav establishing a stable relationship together. Third time lucky had been far from that.

> "I felt tricked and betrayed. He knew the strict and rigorous child custody rules, I didn't. I had been oblivious to the dangers lurking in Norway."
> **Laura in Croatia**

Nicole and Laura's Tips – Divorce and Separation

When dealing with divorce and separation, Laura and Nicole stressed how important it is to:

Finances

- Monitor joint finances.
- Understand how you would cope financially without your partner or if you were out of work.
- Appreciate the legal costs of divorce and separation and gaining custody of your child(ren).

Health

- Recognise that divorce and separation can impact your physical and mental health. For example, overworking to escape issues can lead to health problems.
- Follow your intuition. If something doesn't feel right, it probably isn't.
- Give something back when everything is settled, for example, setting up a support group for people in a similar situation.
- Take time out for yourself to escape reality.
- Find something you are grateful for each day, no matter how small.
- Reward yourself.

Legal

- Invoke the legal system when you no longer trust your partner.
- Adhere to court and authority rulings, for example, child(ren) and parent visiting rights.
- Engage one or more solicitors, realising your case may straddle both your home and host countries.
- Understand your rights in your host country.
  - Do you have the legal right to remain in your host country without your partner?
  - Do you know the child custody regulations in your host country?
- Have a relationship agreement in place, especially when children are involved.

Relationships

- Seek marriage guidance counselling.
- Think twice about entrusting third parties with confidential and sensitive information, for example, a school teacher.
- Reach out to friends and allow them to support you.
- Speak with friends you can trust.
- Push yourself out of your comfort zone. Do activities you previously would never have thought of, for example, going to church.

SINK THEN SWIM

 SWIMMING LESSON TEN
Divorce and Separation

In Swimming Lesson Ten, you are asked to reflect on the divorce and separation stories in this chapter.

1. List below the actions you would take in the event of divorce or separation while living abroad.

2. Research and write below what your legal rights are to remain in your host country without your partner.

Chapter Summary

Storms Don't Last Forever – Divorce and Separation
Sue's Final Comments

When you or your partner want a divorce or to separate, you may feel like you are sinking. However, as you wade through the numerous questions and practicalities requiring your attention, you realise you have a wealth of resources to draw on. These include:

- Learnings from your own integration journey.
- Getting Leggy with any negative, pessimistic and gloomy Thoughts and Emotions.
- The living abroad tips shared in *Chapter Five*.
- The divorce and separation tips shared by Nicole and Laura in this chapter.
- Your own proposed actions on how to deal with divorce and separation detailed in *Swimming Lesson Ten*.

You can manage this, knowing that first you sink and then you swim.

In this chapter you learned …

- Divorce and separation are ugly storms but are storms that don't last forever.
- The importance of having a written relationship agreement if you and your partner are not married.
- The importance of recognising the costs associated with divorce, separation and child custody.
- To instruct a legal representative in both your home and host country when dealing with child custody issues.
- The importance of understanding child custody regulations in your host country.
- To engage a marriage guidance counsellor where necessary.
- The importance of friends for support.

STORMS DON'T LAST FOREVER: DIVORCE AND SEPARATION

In this chapter you have completed one Swimming Lesson.

Congratulate yourself. You've earned your seventh swimming medal.

Useful Resources

- Read *Holding the Fort Abroad.* Rhoda Bangerter. 2001. Summertime Publishing.
- Read 'Is Your Relationship Causing More Pain Than Joy?' Vivian Chiona. https://www.expatnest.com/is-your-relationship-causing-more-pain-than-joy-plus-tips-to-move-forward
- Read *The Art of Coming Home. Chapter One*, Coming Home and *Chapter Two*, The Stages of Reentry. Craig Storti. 2003. Intercultural Press Inc.
- Read *The Family Lawyer's Guide to Separation and Divorce: How to get what you both want.* Laura Naser. 2019. Vermilion.
- Read 'Til stress do us part: the causes and consequences of expatriate divorce'. Yvonne McNulty. Journal of Global Mobility, Vol. 3, No. 2, 2015.
- Watch *Where do I file for divorce if I live in one country and my spouse lives in another?* Diggs and Sadler. https://www.youtube.com/watch?v=Jj1n56yTtM8
- Watch *What if I live abroad and my spouse wants to get divorced?* MensDivorceLawFirm. https://www.youtube.com/watch?v=5J59Sgf-_4A

A Ripple of Laughter

Why did the husband divorce the baker?
Because she was too kneady.

Source: Unknown

CHAPTER EIGHT
Dealing With the Unthinkable: Ill-Health

"Sometimes you have to let go of the picture of what you thought life would be like and learn to find joy in the story you are actually living."

Rachel Marie Martin
American journalist, author, influencer and speaker

Living a Nightmare

- "I knew something wasn't right but chose to ignore the signs."
- "I was too busy to see the doctor."
- "Mum's seriously ill. I need to go home."

These Thoughts, spinning around in your head, begin to haunt you. You wish you'd acted sooner, but now it's too late. The news that you or a relative are ill is undoubtedly unwelcome and distressing. You are dealing with the unthinkable – living a nightmare.

You're all at sea, swirling in Volatility, Uncertainty, Complexity and Ambiguity. You don't know what to do or who to turn to, and waves of fear, anger, confusion, loneliness and sadness wash over you. As the reality of the situation sinks in, you want to know:

- What the diagnosis actually means.
- What medical intervention is proposed and what are the risks?
- The costs of any treatment.
- If time off work is necessary.
- If your or your relative's employer will be supportive.

- How you or your relative will manage financially if you or they are unable to work.
- What the chances of recovery are.
- How long you or your relative have to live.

In her book *Radical Remission*, a book made possible following ten years of research, Kelly A Turner reveals nine topics common to patients who, against all odds, overcame incurable cancer. Three of the nine topics, "taking control of your health", "increasing positive emotions" and "embracing social support" are clear messages to everyone, including you.

In *Chapter Five* you learned that every aspect of your life is impacted by the differences between your home and your host country's culture. Such substantial differences can impact your health. Taking your health seriously is of paramount importance when you live abroad.

When you relocated abroad you likely gave little to no thought to you or your relative becoming seriously ill. I know I didn't, yet during the twenty-two years I have lived abroad, I have dealt with several health issues, my own and those of some family members. Understanding what to do when ill-health impacts Your World is crucial, and even more so when you live abroad.

In the stories that follow, Matilde shares how she dealt with her mother's ill-health, and I share how I dealt – and continue to deal – with my own ill-health.

Find the Best Way to Be Present
Matilde's Story – Ill-Health

In *Chapter Five* we saw how living and working abroad is an integral part of Matilde's life. Living in Brussels and regularly travelling to the UK and parts of Africa for work makes visiting family and friends back home in Italy difficult. She misses them. Matilde's Values and Strengths of adaptability, pragmatism and willingness to learn highlighted in her living abroad story come to the fore once again here – in her account of when her mum, Guiliana, became seriously ill.

When Living Abroad Gets Real

'Mum' displayed on Matilde's phone and it sent shivers down her spine. Something wasn't right. This wasn't the time they usually spoke.

"I'm sorry, Matilde. I have bad news." Her mum's voice was shaking. "The cancer's back."

Sniffles crescendoed as the news sank in, and tears streamed down their faces. The yearning to embrace one another only added to their pain.

Matilde had been just ten years old when her mum was first diagnosed with cancer. "I remember the time vividly," she said with sadness in her eyes. "Treatments were not as advanced as they are nowadays. People were dying." Matilde's Thoughts raced away with her.

It was now 2019. Matilde was living and working in the UK. Her husband, Manuel, was at home in Brussels and her mum was in her homeland, Italy. "This is when the reality of living abroad becomes real," said Matilde. Not being physically with her mum to provide immediate support was a huge wake-up call. Caught in a net of guilt and fear, she felt helpless.

Matilde needed to be with her mum and her brother, Daniele – and soon. "We're very close. Daniele bearing the whole responsibility of caring for Mum alone didn't feel right," she said. With surgery already scheduled, there was little time to act. Finding a way through the Volatility, Uncertainty, Complexity and Ambiguity of the situation meant she had to pull on all her resources.

Book Your Flight

The following morning, Matilde cycled to work early. She needed to speak with her manager before the morning meeting began.

Matilde loved cycling in Norwich, but cycling in the Norfolk countryside to and from work was another matter. Regardless of the direction she took, there was always a headwind. En route, her mind was focused on the conversation she needed to have with her boss. With a shedload of work commitments to fulfil and being relatively new to the organisation, anxiety set in. Would she be able to work away from the office? Was she eligible for paid time off, special leave or sick leave? Several questions needed answering, and she feared her boss wouldn't understand her situation.

Taking in the beauty of the big blue sky hovering over field upon field of wheat as she cycled, her mind drifted. The anxiety and fear began to fizzle away, replaced by a sense of calmness and confidence. *Everything's going to be alright*, the voice in her head said. Matilde was Getting Leggy with her Thoughts and Emotions.

"I totally understand," said her manager. "Book your flight. Be with your mum and your brother. Work from Italy. You know your job inside out, much more than I do." The reaction was more than welcome. And her boss was right: as a management consultant, Matilde could work remotely. The following morning, she flew back to Italy.

Working Flexibly

On the flight home she began juggling her work schedule and re-planning her workload. She didn't need to be available to speak with colleagues between nine and five. Instead, she could work in the evenings and weekends. Doing so meant she could visit her mum in hospital during the day.

Keen to have herself and her manager on the same page, she decided that a do-not-disturb message titled *I'm with Mum today* would protect the times she needed to be offline. As she began typing the message, the pilot's announcement interrupted her line of thought. "The weather in Naples is dry, sunny and eighteen degrees." Matilde stared out of the window. Grey cloud was hanging over London. *It looks bleak but everything's going to be alright*, the little voice in her head repeated.

A Problem Shared Is a Problem Halved

Arriving in Italy was emotional. Seeing her mum and her brother was heartwarming, but an undercurrent of sadness and anxiety surrounded them. There was a mountain ahead to climb. Her mum was seriously ill, and they knew it.

Matilde and Daniele created a plan covering caring responsibilities for when Guiliana would be in hospital and back home recuperating. Focusing on the practicalities not only took their mind off the seriousness of the situation but also stopped their Emotions from bubbling over.

Guiliana's surgery took place in the city where Daniele lived, a one-and-a-half-hour drive from her own home. Matilde stayed at her brother's and visited her mum during the day. Daniele took over from Matilde in the early evening after he'd finished work.

A few days after surgery, Guiliana returned home and Matilde took over the household chores. The time they spent together, chatting about life, going for short walks or simply doing nothing, was priceless. Matilde stayed with her mum for just short of two months.

"I'll be on the first flight if you need me," she said as they said their goodbyes.

Manuel was beaming from ear to ear when Matilde opened the door to their apartment. Despite their daily calls, it was clear he had missed his wife. "Manuel's support is always important to me and especially where family is concerned," she said.

Balancing Act

Guiliana stayed with her son during the twenty consecutive radiotherapy treatments. Having her son by her side was reassuring. Back in the UK, Matilde was feeling guilty. Her mum was tired. The treatments had taken their toll on her energy levels, and she now needed to attend regular check-up appointments.

Matilde flew to Italy at regular intervals to support her mum. She wanted to ensure the information shared during these appointments was understood and that all their questions were addressed. Was the cancer completely gone? Was additional treatment needed? When would she be well enough to return to work?

Flying between Italy, England, Belgium and several African countries was, to put it mildly, exhausting. Juggling her personal and professional life became a balancing act. Nevertheless, supporting her mum remained of paramount importance.

No Regrets

Matilde's dad, a doctor, would normally have taken the lead role in caring for his wife. But as they were no longer married, it became the responsibility of Matilde and Daniele. Matilde knows that had her dad been around, she would have visited her mum less often – something she would have regretted. "Don't underestimate the importance of being there in person. My mum and my brother appreciated me being with them, and for me, being with loved ones always comes first."

Giuliana is now in remission and doing well.

> "Nothing is as important as family. Be physically present with your loved ones in their hour of need."
> **Matilde in Belgium**

Heal from the Inside Out
My Story – Ill-Health

In *Chapter One*, we learned how I was diagnosed with cancer for the second time in 2022. What happened next is revealed in my own story, a story in which my Values and Strengths of adaptability, courage and resilience are once again realised.

Life Sentence

A few days after being told the breast cancer had returned, I was again being put under the microscope, this time for an endoscopy with biopsy. Something suspect, located next to my left lung, had shown up on a PET scan. As the tube was being pushed down my throat to remove tissue for analysis, I put on a brave face, quashing any Thoughts that the cancer may have spread. I was in denial, refusing to accept the seriousness of the situation.

But then I got the phone call. "The cancer is treatable but not curable," the doctor said. "There's nothing more we can do."

The initial treatment plan – chemotherapy, an operation to remove the left breast and radiotherapy – was scrapped. I would instead for the rest of my life be taking medication intended to keep the cancer under control.

Great! Medication equals side effects, I said loudly and sarcastically to myself.

After saying our goodbyes, the phone went dead.

The cancer had metastasised. It had spread to the lung lymph nodes. Hans and I looked at each other in disbelief. There were no words. Not once had I thought the cancer I'd been diagnosed with just five years earlier would return. I'd been thrown overboard. I was mentally at rock-bottom. My World was falling apart. I was staring death in the face, and I was terrified.

A Myriad of Reactions

Sharing the news with family and friends was far from easy. I relived the nightmare over and over as heart-warming and heart-wrenching reactions flooded in:

- "What stage?"
- "My brother had just six months following his diagnosis."
- "You'll get through this. You are strong and positive. You'll be fine."
- "Can I come to see you?"
- "I'm here for you, Sue."

Others said nothing, their silence deafening. I was rapidly learning who my real friends were.

The Never-Ending Need to Know

The internet became my best friend and worst enemy. Reading my medical records and researching treatments, medication side effects and life expectancy statistics was, to put it bluntly, shit, but I did it because I wanted to know if there was the slightest possibility of a cure. Most of all, I wanted to know how long I had to live. I needed certainty.

Interpreting medical terminology in your own language is one thing, but understanding it in Dutch was nigh on impossible. My husband became my translator, and when Emotions became too much for the both of us, with permission, the oncologist appointments were recorded.

From Despair to Hope

In the bowels of Volatility and Uncertainty, simple tasks became enormous and daunting undertakings. I was in no fit state to work, but stopping resulted in anguish. I was self-employed, and not working meant zero income and zero money going into my pension pot. *But you may not even reach pensionable age, so why worry about that?* I said disrespectfully to myself. My Thoughts were raw. I was angry and depleted. I felt I couldn't carry on. And, I confess, at times, I didn't want to. Mentally and physically exhausted, I knew it was time to rest, to do nothing, to just be. And so I cut myself off from the Wider World.

Months later, out of the blue, my scrambled mind suddenly cleared. I Got Leggy with my Thoughts and Emotions. *I'm still here*, I told myself. *I'm not dead yet and I'm damned if this thing called cancer is going to get the better of me.* As the fear and sadness dissipated, the bright, shiny faces of confidence and happiness and my best friend, hope, showed up one by one.

Intuition Guides the Way

On top of the diagnosis, the last thing I needed was to lose weight, but that's exactly what was happening. Stressed and anxious about the cancer and stressed and anxious about losing weight, I was in a vicious circle. Fortunately, after consuming several weight-gain drinks prescribed by a dietician, my weight stabilised.

Like many others diagnosed with cancer, I scrutinised my diet. Drinking more water, eating more cruciferous vegetables, seeds and nuts, and, where possible, obliterating food items containing sugar and simple carbohydrates from my diet became the new norm. However, sensing other factors may have been behind my cancer diagnosis, I stopped and listened to my intuition, which guided me to:

- End my morning shower with sixty seconds of cold water while taking deep breaths and visualising negative Thoughts and Emotions dripping away from me.
- Drink lemon and ginger water daily.

- Take a daily walk at the beach or in the woods with Hans and our dog, Hooch, whatever the weather.
- Dance and sing to an upbeat song – when my energy levels permitted.
- Swim in the outdoor pool with my Dutch neighbour.
- Meditate thirty minutes a day, even if I doze off most of the time.
- Read more self-development books.
- Journal daily what I like about myself and what I am grateful for.
- Attend Reiki sessions and Yin Yoga lessons.

My intuition had steered me to view my health and well-being holistically. Physical, mental and psychological health are, after all, intertwined. I began to feel calmer and more confident about managing my health.

Serious Side Effects

I was grateful to have escaped chemotherapy, radiotherapy and an operation. Nevertheless, there was no escaping the well-known and potentially debilitating side effects of the Aromatase Inhibitor medication. These drugs reduce the oestrogen levels in the body, slowing or stopping the growth of cancer at least, or shrinking or dissolving it at best. However, they say the cancer never entirely disappears.

Oestrogen is essential for bone, heart and cognitive health. Hot flashes set in immediately, followed by some hair loss, dry skin, dry eyes, dizziness and insomnia. Three months later, joint and muscle pain kicked in, and I developed not one but two frozen shoulders. As for high blood pressure, high cholesterol, decrease in bone density, and heart issues, these aren't proactively checked but ought to be.

My health has become a lifelong project, and there's not a day that goes by when I'm not considering how I can improve it. Acutely aware of the five-year expiry date of the Aromatase Inhibitors, I do a daily pep talk as I swallow the medication every evening. "Thank you, Letrozole, for being part of my cancer treatment team. Together we'll at least keep the cancer under control and, at best, we'll eliminate it. Thank you for little to no side effects."

Along with others diagnosed with metastasised breast cancer, I will likely take the medication until it no longer works. Hopefully this will go well beyond the expiry date and preferably to the end of my life.

Pandora's Box Meets Gobbledygook

With spring knocking on the door, it was the perfect time to begin writing that book I'd always promised myself. As I began to write, Pandora's box opened. It was time for some inner work. It was time to face deep-rooted, suppressed childhood trauma. It was time to heal from the inside out.

Inner work? That's all gobbledygook, right? Never before would I have entertained such a thing, but I had nothing to lose, had I? Discussing my Emotions in a foreign language with a Dutch psychologist wasn't easy, but I sensed how pivotal this was for my mental health. For decades I'd been a people pleaser who failed to set boundaries and who regularly sought feedback and recognition from others to prove my worth. Workaholism had ensued, followed by numerous burnouts.

My inner work journey continued, but now at a deeper level. Had I realised beforehand what was involved I may not have embarked on the journey. Allowing my body to feel the pain associated with deep-rooted Emotions – and to release these without judgement – was excruciatingly painful. Outbursts of anger and floods of tears became key features of the bi-weekly somatic healing and counselling sessions.

Healing from the inside out continues to be an arduous yet transformative journey. Deep-rooted, self-sabotaging behaviours linked to my childhood have mostly fizzled away. Recalling events without being emotionally triggered is liberating.

My Health, My Responsibility

"There's nothing more we can do," the medical team had said. And while they could do no more, apart from prescribe Aromatase Inhibitors and conduct three-monthly check-ups (which continue to stir up feelings of anxiety), there was plenty *I* could do. I'm fully aware the cancer *may* have cut my life expectancy and that Uncertainty has become a new norm. Nevertheless, I'm grateful for the opportunity it has sent my way to live each day doing what is important to me. After all, as Abraham Lincoln once said, "It's not the years in your life that count. It's the life in your years." *Me first* has become my daily mantra.

At the time of writing, all four tumours have shrunk and the cancer remains stable. I genuinely believe I am healing from the inside out.

> "Staring death in the face gave me one hell of a jolt, but it also opened a door, a door of opportunity to heal from the inside out and to focus on living my life doing things important to me and that I enjoy."
> **Me (Sue) in the Netherlands**

Tips from Matilde and Me – Ill-Health

When dealing with ill-health, Matilde and I stressed how important it is to:

Finances

- Consider how you would cope financially if you needed to take time off work or were no longer able to work.
- Review sick leave and special leave entitlements.

Health

- Look at your health holistically, namely, your physical, mental and psychological health.
- Be your own advocate:
  - Diet – Engage a dietician, where necessary. Drink water regularly. Reduce or eliminate your intake of sugar and simple carbohydrates.
  - Exercise – Go for a daily walk. Swim. Do yoga. Sing. Dance.
  - Rest – It's OK to do nothing some days, to just *be*.
  - Meditate – Do breathing exercises while visualising negative Thoughts and Emotions seeping away from your body.
- Ask for help to interpret medical terminology.
- Apply caution when researching medical conditions.
- Set boundaries for yourself.
- Work with a psychologist, a somatic healing counsellor, and/or a Reiki practitioner to help you cope with suppressed Emotions and trauma.

- Journal to capture your Thoughts and Emotions and to release inner tensions.

Relationships

- Take someone with you to medical appointments. Ask to record meetings when the information and Emotions become too much.
- Be selective. Don't rush to share ill-health news with others.
- Visit and support your ill relative. You'll likely regret it later if you don't.
- Share caring responsibilities with relatives where possible.
- Attend medical appointments with your ill relative where possible. Take notes and ask questions on their behalf.

Work

- Work fewer hours or stop work completely.
- Take sick leave or special leave as necessary.
- Learn to feel comfortable with your personal life taking precedence over your work life.
- Be open and honest with your employer.
    - Ask for time off to be with your ill relative.
    - Suggest do-not-disturb times during surgery and treatment.
    - Amend your workload and working hours where possible.

DEALING WITH THE UNTHINKABLE: ILL-HEALTH

🏊 SWIMMING LESSON ELEVEN
Ill-Health

In Swimming Lesson Eleven, you are asked to reflect on the ill-health stories in this chapter.

List below the actions you would take if you or a relative became ill while living abroad.

Chapter Summary

Dealing With the Unthinkable – Ill-Health
Sue's Final Comments

When you become ill or receive news that a relative is ill, you may feel like you are sinking. However, as you wade through the numerous questions and practicalities requiring your attention, you realise you have a wealth of resources to draw on. These include:

- Learnings from your own integration journey.
- Getting Leggy with any negative, pessimistic and gloomy Thoughts and Emotions.
- The living abroad tips shared in *Chapter Five*.
- The ill-health tips shared by Matilde and me in this chapter.
- Your own proposed actions for how to deal with ill-health detailed in *Swimming Lesson Eleven*.

You can manage this, knowing that first you sink and then you swim.

In this chapter you learned ...

- To deal with the unthinkable – your ill-health or the ill-health of a relative.
- The importance of reviewing your finances and understanding how you will manage if you aren't able to work.
- Your health is a lifelong project.
- To work with a specialist for mental health and psychological well-being issues. This may include a psychologist, somatic healing counsellor, Reiki practitioner or other professionals.
- Friends may disappear from your life when you share ill-health news.
- The importance of being physically present with your ill relative during surgery, treatments and check-up appointments.

In this chapter you have completed one Swimming Lesson.

Congratulate yourself. You've earned your eighth swimming medal.

Useful Resources

- Look up Kelly Howell's meditation techniques. www.brainsync.com
- Read *How to Do the Work*. Dr Nicole LePera. 2021. Harper Collins.
- Read *Man's Search For Meaning*. Viktor E. Frankl. 2004. Rider.
- Read *Option B*. Sheryl Sandberg and Adam. M. Grant. 2017. Penguin Random House Books.
- Read *Radical Remission: Surviving Cancer Against All Odds*. Chapters Two, Six and Seven. Kelly A. Turner. 2014. Harper Collins.
- Read *Rise: Surviving and Thriving After Trauma*. Sian Williams. 2016. Weidenfeld & Nicolson.
- Read *The Body Keeps the Score*. Bessel van der Kolk. 2015. Penguin Books.
- Read *The Insider's Guide to Metastatic Breast Cancer*. 2019. Anne Loeser. Independently published.
- Read *The PH Miracle*. Dr Robert Young and Dr Sheely Young. 2009. Piatkus.
- Watch *Guided Wim Hof Method Breathing*. Wim Hof. https://www.youtube.com/watch?v=tybOi4hjZFQ&t=19s

A Ripple of Laughter

Where do sick boats go to get healthy?
To the dock.

Source: https://explainthejoke.com/2015/08/15/sea-sick

CHAPTER NINE

In Turbulent Waters: Finding a Job

"I look to the future because that's where I'm going to spend the rest of my life."

George F Burns
American comedian, actor, writer and singer

When One Boat Sails Another One Docks

- "What will I do when I relocate? Where will I work? Can I work?"
- "I never did like it here. I don't fit in."
- "It was time to move on anyway. I just needed a push."

From job searches and job applications to job interviews and job offers, you knew how to navigate your way around finding a job in your homeland. In your host country, however, things are done differently. Finding a job when you live abroad can at best be confusing and at worst destabilising. You want to work. You *need* to work.

You're all at sea, swirling in Volatility, Uncertainty, Complexity and Ambiguity. You don't know what to do or who to turn to, and waves of fear, anger, confusion, loneliness and sadness wash over you. As the reality of the situation sinks in, you want to know:

- Can you legally reside in your host country without a job?
- Can you transfer with your existing employer?
- How long can you afford to be out of work?

- How long will it take to change careers because you can't work in your profession?
- Why your applications are ignored or rejected.
- Why your experience and qualifications are not valued.

"You will have many jobs and even multiple careers in your lifetime," say Bill Burnett and Dave Evans in their book *Designing Your Work Life*. This is particularly pertinent when you live abroad. Your employment journey may be bumpy, hopping from one temporary contract to another. You may also hear that employers hire foreigners mainly where skills shortages exist. Believe this. In some countries this is a well-known yet not openly broadcast fact.

Unless you relocated with a job to go to or had no intention of working when you moved abroad, you likely gave a lot of thought to finding work before you relocated. Similarly, if you find yourself without a job while living abroad, you'll put a lot of thought and effort into finding one quickly. Understanding how to secure a job abroad is critical.

When I emigrated to the USA in 1989, I had a job to go to, but when I relocated to Norway in 2003, there was no job. Qualified and having many years of experience in my profession, I never thought for one minute I would have difficulty securing employment, but I did. In turbulent waters, I discovered that jobs within my profession were limited, and when vacancies appeared, they almost always went to a native. For every job vacancy that sailed away into the distance, my eyes remained wide open, ready for the next one to dock. I persisted and persevered.

In the stories that follow, Evgeny and Hortense share how they dealt with finding a job when relocating and while living abroad.

Looking for a Job Is a Job in Itself
Evgeny's Story – Finding a Job

In *Chapter Five* we met Evgeny, who had for years dreamt of furthering his career in Europe. However, the progress he was making was halted when war broke out between his homeland, Russia, and Ukraine. Evgeny's Values and Strengths of courage, humour and perseverance not only came to the fore in his living abroad story but are once again highlighted here – in his account of finding a job.

No Work Permit, no Job

In 2022, along with four other Russian families, Evgeny and his wife, Helen, emigrated to Turkey with their children, Leo and Julia. Evgeny had no job to go to. By the end of the second year, after all his friends had, one by one, secured employment in Europe, it was Evgeny's turn. But the journey to finding a job in Europe was far from easy.

Realising that no work permits were being issued to Russians in Turkey, Evgeny turned to his ex-employer in Russia. Completing projects remotely from his home in Turkey was a blessing – but a temporary one. When these projects came to an end, he found work with his ex-employer's suppliers. However, this work ended soon after it began when the supply chain in Russia was impacted by the war.

Bespoke or Generic?

After taking Julia to school and walking with Helen and Leo to the local park, Evgeny spent the next four hours in the nearby café sending out the next round of job applications. Glancing up from his laptop from time to time, taking a slurp of tea, he'd look beyond the people sitting outside smoking shisha pipes. Through the rising smoke, he'd spot Helen pushing Leo on the swings. He felt calm.

But not for long. As he looked back at his laptop, two questions were rearing their ugly head.

- Will I get a job?
- How long will it take?

The calmness dissipated, and in its place were frustration and then anger.

"I spent three hours preparing an application for a job in Denmark, and within minutes of pressing the send button, I received a no thank you response." He repeatedly questioned whether he should spend a few minutes sending his generic CV and cover letter or a few hours making his application bespoke. Ploughing through application after application became arduous and soul-destroying.

With no income and a family to support, Evgeny sold some of his investments, but the return was poor. European companies were blocking access to the Russian stock exchange. He turned to his parents. "Can I borrow a few hundred euros?" he asked them. "I need to engage a recruitment agency to help me find a job."

The agency set to work immediately.

Getting Leggy

Evgeny's CV, cover letter and LinkedIn profile were appraised and spruced up. A recruitment tool was then used to match job descriptions with his experience, skills and qualifications. The agency spent an average of forty minutes per job application, but with no interviews forthcoming, Evgeny's anxiety and frustration resurfaced. It was looking less and less likely he'd be able to secure a job. In anger, Evgeny reached out to the agency's Chief Executive Officer, and after another manager was assigned to his case, he started mentoring sessions with professionals working in strategy, production and procurement. With further insights into job titles and job content, his CV and cover letter were updated. Evgeny began to feel calm, his anger having subsided. Three months later, the agency called. He was, at last, being invited to attend interviews. "Used constructively, anxiety, frustration and anger can be a great driver," he said.

Europe on Holiday

"Then everything stopped for the summer," Evgeny said sarcastically. The summer period would last until the end of September. Disheartened, he decided to pursue other options. After speaking with a Russian who had just graduated from Rotterdam School of Management with an MBA, he submitted his application. A week later, his place was confirmed. Evgeny was finally going to Europe and would be starting the MBA programme in January. He was thrilled. What's more, his sister was about to relocate to Rotterdam to study. Things were looking up.

Everybody Out

That same day, the Turkish government announced they were ceasing the residence permit programme for Russians. Without his place on the MBA programme, he and his family would have to return to Russia, something they didn't want to do. Evgeny and Helen immediately applied for Dutch visas for them and the children and began searching for a place to live in the Netherlands.

In early November, the recruitment agency called. Evgeny was being invited to attend not one but two job interviews. Two job offers followed and after some toing and froing of salary negotiations, he signed an employment contract to become a Category Manager of Procurement for an international company based in Germany. It was March 2024.

His place at Rotterdam School of Management was put on hold.

"You need to go to Russia and wait for your visa," a representative from his soon-to-be employer's relocation company said. Evgeny was adamant this wasn't going to happen. Knowing full well returning to Russia was too risky, he contacted the visa centre in Istanbul.

Evgeny and Helen checked the status of their German visa applications daily. Days turned into weeks until one day, out of the blue, Helen received a call. Documents concerning the custody of Julia, the daughter from her first marriage, were needed. Helen was distraught. Frantically riffling through the family's official documents she had gathered before leaving Russia, she quickly realised the documents needed by the German authorities didn't exist in Russia. Their relocation was now in jeopardy.

Helen sent the one and only document she had – the divorce court decision – and to their huge relief, within days, their German visas were ready for collection. They had the green light to live in Europe.

Dream Fulfilled

"It's been hard, but thankfully I have a good sense of humour, and this has saved the day on many occasions," Evgeny said. He and Helen had been going crazy with fear and anxiety. But they'd managed to push themselves to view things in a light-hearted way. Laughing at the countless obstacles they'd encountered had been an absolute must.

After fleeing Russia, Volatility, Uncertainty, Complexity and Ambiguity were thrown at Evgeny from all angles: no work visa, no job, and a family to support. Securing employment in Europe had been no small task. Yet despite the challenges, Evgeny had pushed forward. His courage, perseverance and maintaining a clear picture of why he was doing what he was doing had motivated him to fulfil his dream of working in Europe.

Evgeny appreciates that life in Germany may not one hundred percent meet his expectations, but he intends to integrate into German society and live there long-term. He smiled. "I'm looking forward to taking my family to all the places I've longed to visit. I love mountains and green cities. The German Alps, the Black Forest Mountains, Munich, Cologne, Berlin, they're all on our list. Europe has been a long time coming, but it's finally here," he said.

> "I had a job back home in Russia. Life was easier and more convenient. In Turkey I learned how important support from family and friends is to achieving my professional goals."
> **Evgeny in Turkey**

Starting From Zero
Hortense's Story – Finding a Job

In *Chapter Five* we learned that Hortense, who is originally from the USA, had from a young age wanted to live in Europe. She is, at the time of writing, living in Norway. Her Values and Strengths of courage, perseverance and willingness to learn came to the fore in her living abroad story and are once again highlighted in this finding a job story.

Job Hopping

Hortense's right to reside in Norway was dependent on her having a job. Constantly searching for and applying for work was frustrating and exhausting.

During the first three years of her residency, she submitted a visa application every three to six months and accepted jobs she knew wouldn't be a good match. "Market research, accounting, and IT project work didn't light my fire, but I couldn't be picky about what I did," she said. Her self-worth crashed knowing that back in the USA she would have held a position with a decent salary doing what she loved – working with artists, start-up organisations and emerging markets.

However, in some ways, hopping from one job to another suited Hortense. "When things remain the same, I get bored," she said. Short-term contracts, resignations and redundancy became a prominent feature of Hortense's working life in Norway.

Language Barrier

Hortense identified the skills being sought by employers in jobs that interested her. If she didn't have the appropriate skills, she highlighted alternative, compensatory skills in her job applications. But with employers failing to see the value of her education and experience, her applications continued to be rejected. "I just didn't get it," she said to her friends. But the answer became blatantly obvious. Over seventy percent of job vacancies required a good to excellent command of Norwegian. Through her connections, she Got Leggy, turning confusion into clarity.

Four years after moving to Norway, Hortense secured her first permanent employment contract and was granted a permanent work visa. As the joint owner and manager of an organisation supporting people to establish their own businesses, she was doing exactly what she loved and was good at.

Hortense now wanted to buy her own home and for that she needed a bank loan.

Misfit

She knew that obtaining a bank loan to buy a house would be challenging, particularly as she worked in the private sector – something the banks viewed as a relatively high risk when compared to the public sector. Hortense had had limited experience in the public sector, but undeterred, she pushed forward in the hope of finding a new job.

The timing was perfect. The public sector was being tasked with employing a diverse workforce. Hortense was an immigrant. She also had knowledge and experience within start-ups, organisations needing to secure patents for their ideas, designs, trademarks and inventions. The national industrial property rights organisation was in the public sector. Her immigrant status, start-up knowledge and experience plus her now almost fluent Norwegian, were her way in, and she succeeded.

As the new manager, she asked her team, "What would you like me to do to support you?" The replies were blunt. "I don't need a boss and I don't need support." Hortense was quickly learning how independent Norwegians were. As she'd envisaged, the organisation and the work were, for her, a bad fit. And even though her bank loan application was successful, she was on the lookout for another job once again.

Opening Doors

Having lived in Norway for fourteen years, Hortense now had a substantial network. Many of her contacts had jobs in international organisations, jobs like those they'd had back home. She longed for something similar and asked her network of friends to keep their eyes and ears open for any job openings. Soon after, a friend of a friend got in contact. A position was about to be advertised but at a lower level than the grade Hortense was looking for. "I can do this," she said at the interview, "but can the job title be changed?" The position had been newly created, so Hortense believed there was a chance she'd get her wish. After negotiating the contractual terms, Hortense received a job offer – and with the job title she'd asked for. Not long afterwards she was promoted to global IT manager.

This time, Hortense decided to push the boat out. She wanted to celebrate her promotion with friends. The sun was still shining high in the sky as she gazed across Oslo harbour towards Akershus Fortress, where a huge cruise ship had docked for the night. It was the height of summer and extremely busy. Friends and lovers linked arms, attempting to stay upright having had too much to drink, and others simply strolled by, licking ginormous multi-flavoured ice creams. Her line of sight returned to her friends chatting and laughing. Hortense was content. Life was good.

Giving Back

From the outset, Hortense was keen to provide career opportunities to foreigners in the same situation she'd been in. She began recruiting talented professionals that other employers were turning a blind eye to. Those who wanted to progress moved on quickly within the organisation after previously cautious managers began to see the potential they had.

Three years in, monotony set in. Hortense approached her manager to discuss her next career move. Discussions with the HR department began immediately. Unbeknown to her, her department had been targeted for restructuring, and HR were looking for volunteers to leave. Negotiations began and soon afterwards she signed her exit package. She left without a job to go to. "I was done and knew I could take the risk," she said.

Way Too Long

Shortly after leaving, Hortense was approached by head-hunters, something that had never happened before. After almost twenty years of living in Norway, her experience and qualifications were finally being valued. "It's a real shame it took so long. You start from zero as a foreigner," she groaned.

Hortense was greeted with Volatility, Uncertainty, Complexity and Ambiguity when finding work in Norway. Not only had her right to reside been dependent on her having a job, but she also had to resort to taking jobs that fell short of her talents. She had this advice for anyone looking to work abroad: "Don't fixate on a specific job title, organisation or industry. Instead, focus on what you want to do, and along the way take advantage of opportunities that present themselves."

"We have paranoia in the USA," she continued. "With few employment rights in many states, you can lose your job at any moment. Americans are advised to have three to six months' savings to cover any potential periods of unemployment. Hortense's American background had put her in good stead to handle the turbulent journey she encountered finding work in Norway.

> "I get bored easily. Variety in my work is crucial. I don't view looking for work as stressful, I view it instead as an opportunity to learn new things."
> **Hortense in Norway**

Evgeny and Hortense's Tips – Finding a Job

When dealing with finding a job, Evgeny and Hortense stressed how important it is to:

Finances

- Review your finances. Identify ways to generate and save money when you are not earning.
- Ask relatives for help.
- Have at least three to six months of savings to cover any period of unemployment.

Health

- Recognise when a job and/or organisation aren't right for you.
- Know your limits and when to delegate some of the job search and application process.
- Appreciate that it will likely take you longer to secure employment in your host country than in your home country.

Legal

- Check if you can work in your host country.
- Check how long you can legally stay in your host country without work.
- Know your employment rights. For example, if you are dismissed through redundancy or otherwise, is it possible to negotiate an exit package?

Relationships

- Share your experiences with friends. Doing so may provide insights into why your applications are not successful.
- Engage your network in your job search.
- Celebrate your successes with friends.

Work

- Continue to work with your existing employer where possible.
- Ask suppliers of your employer if they are recruiting.
- Structure your days to focus entirely on your job search and applications.
- Understand the job market, specifically, skills being sought by employers.
- Identify alternative, complementary skills in the event you don't have the skills being sought by employers.
- Match your experience, qualifications and skills to the content of the job advertisements.
- Recognise how holiday periods can affect the job market.
- Work with a mentor.
- Engage recruitment agencies to assist with your job search and applications.
- Learn the language.
- Be adaptable.
  - Accept short-term contracts.
  - Consider industry sectors, organisations and jobs outside of your experience.
  - Consider further education as an alternative to working.
  - Negotiate job offers.

SWIMMING LESSON TWELVE
Finding a Job

In Swimming Lesson Twelve, you are asked to reflect on the finding a job stories in this chapter.

Imagine yourself searching for work while living abroad. List below what you would do to secure a job.

Chapter Summary

In Turbulent Waters – Finding a Job
Sue's Final Comments

When you are looking for a job, you may feel like you are sinking. However, as you wade through the numerous questions and practicalities requiring your attention, you realise you have a wealth of resources to draw on. These include:

- Learnings from your own integration journey.
- Getting Leggy with any negative, pessimistic and gloomy Thoughts and Emotions.
- The living abroad tips shared in *Chapter Five*.
- The finding a job tips shared by Evgeny and Hortense in this chapter.
- Your own proposed actions of how to find a job detailed in *Swimming Lesson Twelve*.

You can manage this, knowing that first you sink and then you swim.

In this chapter you learned ...

- When you are searching for a job abroad you may feel like you are in turbulent waters.
- To be flexible on your career journey.
- To engage family, friends and recruitment agencies in your job search.
- To have savings in place to fall back on.
- Securing employment of a similar status to what you have in your home country can take time, sometimes years. Be patient.

In this chapter you have completed one Swimming Lesson.

Congratulate yourself. You've earned your ninth swimming medal.

Useful Resources

- Read *A Career in Your Suitcase*. Jo Parfitt and Colleen Reichrath-Smith. 2013. Summertime Publishing.

- Read *Career Jump*. Dorota Klop-Sowinska. 2019. D&R Coaching Consulting. Self-published.
- Read 'Cover Letters – Missed Opportunities'. Sue Schoormans. https://sueschoormansauthor.com/blog/cover-letters-missed-opportunities
- Read *Designing Your Work Life*. Bill Burnett and Dave Evans. 2020. Penguin Random House.
- Read 'Going It Alone'. Sue Schoormans. https://sueschoormansauthor.com/blog/going-it-alone
- Read 'Network, Network, Network'. Sue Schoormans. https://sueschoormansauthor.com/blog/network-network-network
- Read *Own Your Career*. Drake Elliott. 2020. Self-published.
- Read 'State of the Global Workplace 2023 Report'. https://www.gallup.com/workplace/506879/state-global-workplace-2023-report.aspx
- Read 'What do I want to be when I grow up'. Sue Schoormans. https://sueschoormansauthor.com/blog/what-do-I-want-to-be-when-I-grow-up?

A Ripple of Laughter

I lost my job as an ice cream tester.
I couldn't do sundaes.

Source: https://barrypopik.com/blog/just_been_sacked_as_an_ice

PART FOUR

ON THE CREST OF A WAVE

> "Knowing others is intelligence; knowing yourself is true wisdom. Mastering others is strength; mastering yourself is true power."

Lao Tzu
Chinese philosopher famous for Taoism

CHAPTER TEN

Mastering Swimming Strokes: Developing Values and Strengths

"A smooth sea never made a skilled sailor."
Franklin D. Roosevelt
Longest serving American President

Gain Even More Confidence, Calmness, Clarity, Connections and Happiness

Hands up if, like me, you've ever spent a full day – maybe half a day – sitting in a room being talked at. Training courses used to be delivered in stuffy classrooms and, in some cases, still are. When you consider that the average concentration span is around twenty minutes, you can immediately see how ineffective this is. The reality is, we learn mostly from experience, by rolling our sleeves up and doing. As Richard Branson, a business tycoon, once said, "You don't learn to walk by following the rules. You learn by doing and falling over." Learning can take place in many ways and many settings, including working with others to solve problems, delivering a presentation, working with a mentor, handling complaints, and making a mistake or two.

So far in this book you have been learning by reading and answering questions in the *Swimming Lessons*. But in this chapter, you'll learn by doing. As you practise what you commit to in *Swimming Lesson Thirteen*, you'll gain even more confidence, calmness, clarity, connections and happiness and will subsequently be better equipped to deal with life's most stressful situations when living abroad.

In *Part Three*, the stories shared by Anna, Evgeny, Hortense, Laura, Matilde, Nicole, Pauline and me revealed how certain Values and Strengths can help deal with life's most stressful situations. These are:

- Adaptability
- Connections (including Listening, Observation and Questioning skills)
- Courage
- Humour
- Integrity
- Listening Skills
- Observation Skills
- Perseverance
- Pragmatism
- Questioning Skills
- Resilience
- Willingness to Learn

In this chapter we'll look at how to develop each of these as your own.

Defining and Developing Values and Strengths

Defining specific Values and Strengths is as simple as looking up their meaning in a dictionary. However, many words have different meanings depending upon the context in which they're used. This is where a thesaurus can help. For example, later in this chapter you'll see that *courage* – defined as 'facing adversity and the unknown with confidence' – has the synonyms of Boldness, Bravery and Nerve.

Once you're clear on the meaning of specific Values and Strengths, the next step is to realise the level of competency and confidence you have for each of these. Plotting each in a Competence (performance) and Confidence (enjoyment) Matrix, as shown overleaf, enables you to easily see this.

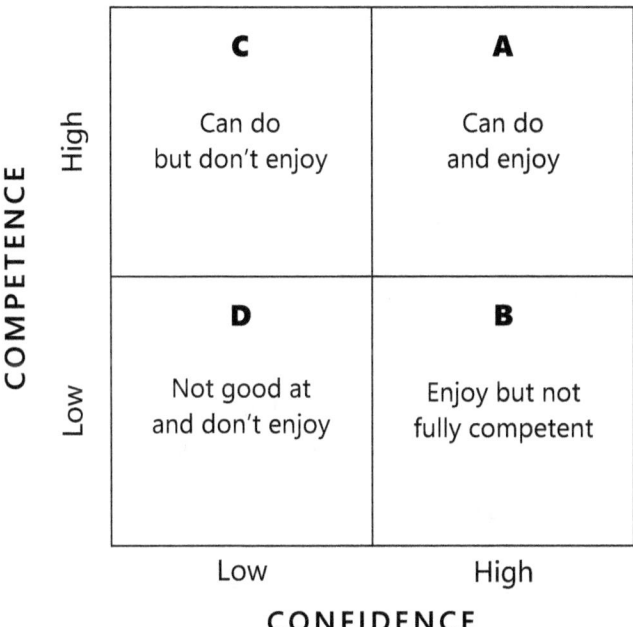

Fig. 10.1 – Competence and Confidence Matrix
The Strengths Profile Model of Development, modified with permission of Cappfinity, owners of the Strengths Profile.

In the matrix:

- Box A depicts Values and Strengths you are good at and enjoy. If you overuse these, however, you may start to enjoy them less and they could fall into box C.
- Box B depicts Values and Strengths where your competence is mediocre and your confidence high. Using these more often increases competence. Consequently, they can move to Box A.
- Box C depicts Values and Strengths in which you are competent but not confident. To avoid further depletion of your confidence, use these only when necessary. They may then move to Box A.
- Box D depicts what you are not good at and don't enjoy. These are your Weaknesses. As a reminder, Weaknesses are covered in *Chapter Four*.

After identifying your levels of competence and confidence for specific Values and Strengths, you can then move on to develop those located in box B and box C and to develop further those located in box A.

There are several overarching ways to develop your Values and Strengths, including:

- Learn more about them. Read books on the subject. Do an internet search.
- Observe and mirror others using them.
- Speak with and question others who use them.
- Practise, practise, practise.
- Ask others to observe you using them and to give you feedback.
- Reward your progress. (See *Chapter Eleven* for more about rewards.)
- Reflect regularly on:
  - How you feel when using the Value or Strength.
  - What is going well.
  - What can be improved.

In the following pages, we'll take a look at the specific Values and Strengths highlighted in *Chapter Five*: how they are defined, how to develop each one as your own or to further develop any which are already yours, and how the living abroad stories show them in action.

ADAPTABILITY

"The only way to make sense out of change is to plunge into it, move with it, and join the dance."
Alan Watts
British-born American philosopher

Definition

Adjusting to something new or different with ease.

Synonyms

Change; Modification; Versatility.

How To Develop Adaptability

Go with the flow by living in the here and now.

Expect and accept Volatility, Uncertainty, Complexity and Ambiguity as part of life.

View change as an opportunity rather than a threat.

Challenge yourself to do new things.

Act without having the full picture.

View failure as an opportunity to learn and to improve.

Accept people, places and circumstances for who and what they are:
- *Avoid judging others.*
- *Avoid making assumptions.*
- *Listen to and consider the views of others.*

Be flexible in your thinking, your habits and your actions.

Be open to new ways of doing things:

- *Do what you do but in a different way.*
- *Change your routine(s), even if only in a small way.*

Observe and copy others who are adaptable.

Ask others how they develop adaptability.

As a reminder, in *Chapters One, Two, Five, Six* and *Eight*, Matilde, Pauline and I demonstrated *adaptability* in the following ways:

I ...

- Reinstated my EU citizenship by becoming a Dutch citizen following the Brexit referendum.
- Got in the car and drove in Norway despite having to drive on the right.
- Modified my behaviours in Norway by looking at how the locals behaved.
- Identified where improvements could be made to my health and embedded these into my daily life.

Matilde ...

- Initiated conversations with strangers.
- Used her language skills to speak with other internationals.
- Dropped everything to be with her mum after the cancer diagnosis.
- Juggled her work schedules and re-planned her workload to care for her mum during and after surgery.
- Flew back and forth from Italy to continue supporting her mum after her treatment ended.

Pauline ...

- Grasped the opportunity to start afresh when she moved to the Netherlands.
- Embraced who she is – the funny, emotionally expressive Spanish girl.
- Flew back and forth from Spain to the Netherlands to care for her dying dad and later to handle both his and her mum's passing.
- Put a boundary in place when her dad's behaviour became abusive.
- Temporarily moved to Spain with her family and dog when her dad was dying and her mum was in hospital.

CONNECTIONS

"There are good ships and wood ships, ships that sail the sea; the best ships are friendships, may they always be."
Irish proverb

Definition

Reaching out and interacting with others. Humans are, after all, social animals.

Synonyms

Association; Communication; Relationships.

How To Develop Connections

Reach out to others:

- *Seek friendly faces.*
- *Begin a conversation with a stranger.*
- *Begin a conversation with someone you wouldn't normally speak with.*
- *Build a support network to develop friendships.*
- *Don't be afraid to ask for help.*

Build rapport. Find common ground with others:

- *Show interest in others.*
- *Show interest in the new and unfamiliar.*
- *Be open and receptive to what others have to say.*
- *Actively listen.*
- *Observe.*
- *Ask questions.*
- *Speak clearly, alternating your tone and volume.*
- *Acknowledge the feelings and Emotions of others.*

Interact with others:

- *Get involved with local community events and groups of interest.*

- *Participate in conversations.*
- *Share your opinions and views by saying what you think and feel.*

Be open-minded. Avoid judging and making assumptions.

Build relationships with people who share your Values and your motivation to do things and those who don't.

Be your authentic self.

Observe and copy others who connect well with others.

Ask others how they develop connections.

As a reminder, in *Chapters Five, Six* and *Seven*, Anna, Laura and Nicole demonstrated connections in the following ways:

Anna ...
- Joined networking events and hobby groups.
- Connected with the locals and made new friends by observing and copying their behaviours.
- Socialised with others to learn about the culture.
- Worked tirelessly to maintain friendships all over the world.
- Kept in contact with her cousin's daughter, Carol, after Abigail's passing.
- Intends to meet with Abigail's colleagues when she next visits the USA to learn more about her cousin.

Laura ...
- Socialised with locals while exploring her host country as a tourist.
- Established new friendships with locals and internationals at networking events.
- Established new friendships with churchgoers.

Nicole ...
- Developed new friendships by joining networking groups and doing volunteer work.
- Established a sisterhood of friends.

COURAGE

"Courageous people stay true to themselves, take risks, face challenges head-on, and lead by example."
Franziska Iseli
Author of *The Courage Map*

Definition

Facing adversity and the unknown with confidence.

Synonyms

Boldness; Bravery; Nerve.

How To Develop Courage

Embrace FEAR – Face Everything And Rise.

- *Get Leggy. Turn your fear into confidence.*
- *Face challenges head-on.*

Be bold:

- *Explore the unknown by stepping out of your comfort zone.*
- *Jump right in. Don't hold back and don't procrastinate.*
- *Push yourself forward to experience the untried and untested.*

Experiment:

- *Do new things.*
- *Do things in a different way.*
- *Change your routines and habits.*
- *Repeat things that didn't go well first time around but in a different way.*
- *Continuously seek improvements.*

Don't give in:

- *Don't be afraid to challenge or disagree with others.*
- *Speak out. Say what needs to be said. Say what you believe to be right.*

Believe in yourself. Say to yourself, *I can do this.*

Observe and copy others who are courageous.

Ask others how they develop courage.

As a reminder, in *Chapters Two*, *Five*, *Eight* and *Nine*, Evgeny, Hortense and I demonstrated *courage* in the following ways:

Evgeny ...

- Left his home country under a cloud of Uncertainty, with no home and no job to go to.
- Sold some of his investments to support his family.
- Asked his parents for money to engage a recruitment company.
- Refused to return to Russia to wait for German visas.

Hortense ...

- Pointed out to the locals that some things were done differently beyond their country's border.
- Walked quickly and calmly away from a potentially threatening situation.
- Applied for and secured jobs in sectors where she had little previous experience.
- Resigned from jobs she felt no longer benefited her, despite having no job to go to.

I ...

- Considered the prospect of working in the USA scary, but nothing was going to get in the way of this once in a lifetime opportunity.
- Emigrated to Norway to live with my new partner and simultaneously left my job and sold my home.
- Wasn't afraid to handle deep-rooted, suppressed Emotions linked to childhood trauma in my quest to manage metastasised breast cancer.

HUMOUR

"A day without laughter is a day wasted."
Charlie Chaplin
English actor, filmmaker and composer famous for silent films

Definition

Viewing things in a light-hearted and laughable way.

Synonyms

Amusement; Fun; Hilarity.

How To Develop Humour

Smile.

Be cheerful.

Be enthusiastic about life.

Allow yourself to have fun.

View things in a light-hearted way.

See the funny side of things.

Laugh to ease pressure, stress and anxiety.

Read and tell jokes.

Read and share funny stories.

Make a joke of any difficult or stressful situation.

Laugh at yourself.

Laugh with others.

Watch your favourite comedians.

Watch comedy programmes and movies.

Observe and copy others who use humour during difficult times.

Observe and copy others who are naturally funny.

Ask others how they develop humour.

As a reminder, in *Chapters Five*, *Seven* and *Nine*, Evgeny and Laura demonstrated *humour* in the following ways:

Evgeny ...

- Giggled and smiled at some of the Turkish habits.
- Laughed when referring to his wife as a bureaucratic monster.
- Appreciated his sense of humour and discovered that looking at things in a light-hearted way helped save the day on many occasions.

Laura ...

- Laughed at some of the cultural peculiarities she encountered in Norway and Spain.
- Used humour as a coping mechanism when dealing with gaining custody of her son.
- Smiled at Sinnataggen, the little boy famous for his determined posture and angry look, when walking in Oslo's famous sculpture park.

INTEGRITY

*"Integrity is doing the right thing,
even when no one is watching."*
CS Lewis
British writer, literary scholar and theologist

Definition

Being honest with yourself and others. Adhering to your moral and ethical standards.

Synonyms

Honesty; Honour; Morality.

How To Develop Integrity

Say what you mean and mean what you say.

Act in alignment with your Values and what you believe to be right.

Keep your promises.

Keep things confidential that should remain confidential.

Consider the impact of your decisions and actions on others.

Demonstrate learning from mistakes:

- *Admit to them – and promptly.*
- *Say sorry.*
- *Identify what you would do differently next time around.*

Observe and copy others who demonstrate integrity.

Ask others how they develop integrity.

As a reminder, in *Chapters Five* and *Seven*, Laura and Nicole demonstrated *integrity* in the following ways:

Laura and Nicole …

- Understood the importance of getting to grips with and adapting to their host country's cultures while never losing sight of their authentic selves.

Laura …

- Moved to Norway knowing it was the right thing to do for her partner, Olav, and her son, Jakov.
- Hired two solicitors (a Croatian and a Norwegian) to manage her child custody case.

Nicole …

- Remained her authentic self by holding on to her Canadian Values.
- Filed for divorce when she learned of her husband's deceit and infidelity.
- Along with her husband, informed their daughter's school teacher of their intention to divorce.
- Started a support group to show her appreciation for the help she had received from her friends during her divorce proceedings.

LISTENING SKILLS

"When people talk listen completely. Don't be thinking what you're going to say. Most people never listen."
Ernest Hemingway
American novelist, writer and journalist

Definition

Paying attention to what is being said.

Synonyms

Alert; Concentration; Taking notice.

How To Develop Listening Skills

Be silent and actively concentrate when someone is speaking. The word *silent* uses the same letters as *listen*.

Give your undivided attention when someone is speaking.

Seek to understand what is being said.

Listen to voice tone and speed. Know it's not only about what is being said but also how.

Close your mind to stop your opinions from seeping through.

Don't interrupt. Allow the person speaking to finish what they are saying before responding.

Be patient and open to views different from your own.

Take notes where necessary.

Show interest in what is being said by:

- *Maintaining eye contact.*
- *Nodding.*
- *Shaking your head.*
- *Leaning forward.*

Come across as friendly and cooperative by:

- *Looking at the other person.*
- *Smiling and mirroring the speaker's facial expression.*
- *Not crossing your arms.*

Come across as thoughtful by:

- *Tilting your head slightly to one side.*
- *Standing still.*
- *Placing your hand on your chin or cheek if sitting down.*

Understand:

- *Errors in speech may be due to stress and anxiety.*
- *Words used can relate to the speaker's attitude towards the subject.*

Reflect, paraphrase and mirror back what you have heard to check your understanding. For example, "As I understand it, you are wanting to …"

Observe and copy others who listen attentively.

Ask others how they develop listening skills.

As a reminder, in *Chapter Five*, Hortense, Matilde and Nicole demonstrated *listening skills* in the following ways:

Hortense …

- Identified where the emphasis is placed in the language by listening to and analysing the behaviours of locals.
- Spoke with friends and joined networking groups in order to understand the behaviours of locals.

Matilde …

- Identified language nuances when communicating in English.

Nicole …

- Identified the brutally honest communication style of the locals by listening to what they were saying and how.

OBSERVATION SKILLS

"To acquire knowledge, one must study; but to acquire wisdom, one must observe."
Marilyn vos Savant
American magazine columnist

Definition

Actively paying attention to what others are doing.

Synonyms

Monitoring; Reviewing; Watching.

How To Develop Observation Skills

Consciously look at what is going on around you.

Notice and interpret facial expressions. They reveal emotional states.

Interpret the body language of others:

- *Nodding unnecessarily may mean loss of interest.*
- *Pulling the ear may mean uncertainty or indecisiveness.*
- *Touching the nose may mean doubt, not telling the truth or covering up Emotions.*
- *Covering the mouth may mean thinking or holding something back.*
- *Resting the chin on the hand may mean deep thinking and evaluating.*
- *Touching fingertips may mean analysing.*
- *Clasped hands may mean anxiety.*
- *Arms crossed may mean reserved, defensive, not convinced or being physically cold.*
- *Leaning forward may mean being interested and actively listening.*
- *Leaning backwards may mean confident and attentive listening.*

Be aware:

- *Eye contact for too long can feel uncomfortable.*
- *Eye contact in some cultures is avoided.*
- *Being too near to someone may feel uncomfortable.*

Be conscious of your own behaviours. What do you notice?

Observe and copy the behaviours of others who observe well.

Ask others how they develop observation skills.

As a reminder, in *Chapters Two* and *Five*, Anna, Hortense, Nicole and I demonstrated *observation skills* in the following ways:

Anna ...

- Connected with the locals and made new friends by observing and copying their behaviours.

Hortense ...

- Identified where the emphasis is placed in the language by observing and analysing the behaviours of locals.

I ...

- Modified my behaviours in Norway after observing those of the locals.

Nicole ...

- Observed the behaviours of locals and in doing so noticed that these collided with her own ways of doing things.

PERSEVERANCE

> *"May you never forget that when it was hard, and you were overwhelmed, and felt afraid, and walked alone, and felt invisible, and didn't have the answers, and couldn't see the way, and wanted to give up ... you kept going."*
> **Nakeia Homer**
> American well-being educator and self-care author

Definition

Keeping going. Not stopping.

Synonyms

Endurance; Persistence; Tenacity.

How To Develop Perseverance

Focus on the bigger picture.

Understand that the journey is as pivotal as – or even more important than – the destination.

View your living abroad journey as a learning opportunity.

Do something you keep putting off.

Don't give up. Commit to your intentions.

- *Focus on what is relevant and discard what isn't.*
- *Eliminate distractions.*
- *Work through obstacles.*
- *Move to plan B if plan A doesn't work. Move to plan C if plan B doesn't work, and so on.*
- *Understand that if at first you don't succeed, try again.*
- *Be aware things may take longer than you expect.*
- *See things through to their conclusion unless it isn't feasible to do so.*

Learn to feel comfortable with the uncomfortable.

Be sensitive to and tolerant of others and their views.

Listen and don't interrupt others when they speak.

Observe and copy others who persevere.

Ask others how they develop perseverance.

As a reminder, in *Chapters Five*, *Six* and *Nine*, Evgeny, Hortense and Pauline demonstrated *perseverance* in the following ways:

Evgeny ...

- Persisted with opening a bank account despite initially being told this wasn't possible.
- Found being in nature helped him remain focused on his dream of working in Europe.
- Moved to plan B, hiring a recruitment agency to search for and apply for jobs when writing application after application became arduous and soul-destroying.

Hortense ...

- Researched the economy and the educational requirements of several countries before deciding where to emigrate to.
- Completed a master's degree knowing this would help her get a job in Europe.
- Hopped from one job to another to retain her right to reside in Norway.
- Searched for work in the public sector, a sector where she had little experience.

Pauline ...

- Developed friendships with other internationals after discovering that making friends with locals who had never lived abroad was difficult.
- Kept going despite repeated challenges – the declining health of her dad, his death, and the passing of her mum.

PRAGMATISM

"Knowing yourself, knowing where you want to get, combining those things gives you the pragmatic steps."
John Amaechi
English-American organisational psychologist and author

Definition

Doing something in a practical as opposed to theoretical way.

Synonyms

Logic; Practicality; Realism.

How To Develop Pragmatism

Identify the problem before setting about resolving what you think the problem is.

- *Analyse the situation and ask questions to identify the root cause.*
- *Do some research to obtain the facts.*
- *Look beyond the obvious.*
- *Identify links between unrelated matters.*

Seek assistance and support to solve the problem.

Create a plan covering all aspects of what you are managing.

Focus on what needs to be done.

Organise and prioritise what needs to be done.

Be eager and enthusiastic to get things done.

- *Don't let problems fester.*
- *Avoid procrastination.*

Realise there will never be a perfect time to do something. Now is good enough.

Admit you may not have all the answers.

Monitor your progress towards achieving your goals.

Keep learning new things.

Observe and copy others who are pragmatic.

Ask others how they develop pragmatism.

As a reminder, in *Chapters Five, Six, Seven* and *Eight*, Anna, Matilde and Nicole demonstrated *pragmatism* in the following ways:

Anna:

- Researched her soon-to-be host country before relocating.
- Immersed herself in her local community soon after relocating, knowing that socialising was critical to her integration.
- Telephoned and wrote letters to her cousin Abigail when she was unable to travel to see her.
- Shared photos of her and Abigail at Abigail's memorial service.

Matilde:

- Spoke with locals to understand which areas were safe to run in.
- Rented a room in a shared house to save money and to avoid being tied to a long-term contract.
- Amended her work schedule and workload during her mum's cancer treatment.
- Along with her brother, created a plan covering caring responsibilities for their mum.

Nicole:

- Decided to get to grips with her host country's culture before starting to learn the language.
- Plans to live with her friends in old age.
- Along with her husband, informed their daughter's teacher of their pending divorce.
- Set up a support group for women facing divorce, separation or loss of their partner.

QUESTIONING SKILLS

"The power to question is the basis of all human progress."
Indira Gandhi
First female Indian Prime Minister

Definition

Seeking answers to your queries using all your senses – what you see, hear, feel, smell, taste and sense.

Synonyms

Curiosity; Flexibility, Resolve.

How To Develop Questioning Skills

Ask open questions to:

- *Establish rapport.*
- *Obtain comprehensive information.*
- *Gain clarity.*
- *Understand someone's viewpoint and feelings.*

> Note: Open questions begin with What, Why and How and, to a lesser extent, Who, When, Where. For example, *How do you know that?*

Ask closed questions to:

- *Obtain a one-word answer. For example, a Yes or a No.*

> Note: Closed questions may begin with a verb. For example, *Do* you need this? They may also begin with a question word. For example, *Where* do you live?

Combine open and closed questions to dig deep by using the funnel or probing technique:

- *Begin with a series of open questions, for example, How do you know that? How do you feel about it? Why does this matter to you?*
- *Then, ask a closed question, for example, Do you think this was the best approach? This may be your final question or you may then return to further open questions; for example, Why do you think this was the best approach?*
- *Finally, end with a closed question, for example, Are you satisfied with the outcome?*

> Note: Be aware that both the person asking and the person answering may find this technique uncomfortable. It will, however, almost always get to the core of the matter being addressed.

Ask reflective questions to:

- *Demonstrate you have been listening.*
- *Summarise what has been said.*
- *Get the person to self-reflect.*

For example, You've said you're an introvert and that asking questions doesn't come naturally to you. How do you cope with this?

Be concise and specific when asking questions.

Avoid:

- *Leading questions. These questions imply the answer and a desired response. For example, This is better, don't you think?*
- *Multiple questions. This question contains more than one question. You will either get an answer to the first or the last question. For example, Global warming is a myth, isn't it? Or do you agree with what the scientists say?*

Observe and copy others who question others well.

Ask others how they develop questioning abilities.

As a reminder, in *Chapters Five* and *Eight*, Hortense, Matilde and I demonstrated *questioning skills* in the following ways:

Hortense ...

- Sought answers to why the locals did what they did.

I ...

- Sought answers to countless questions about my ill-health despite not liking some of the answers I got.

Matilde ...

- Spoke with locals to ascertain safe areas in which to run.
- Asked locals for directions even if she already knew where she was going.
- Went with her mum to her check-up appointments, asking questions to get clarity about the treatment programme.

RESILIENCE

> *"Our greatest weakness lies in giving up. The most certain way to succeed is always to try just one more time."*
> **Thomas Edison**
> American inventor and businessman famous for inventing the lightbulb

Definition

Surviving and then resuming normal life after setbacks.

Synonyms

Determination; Resolve; Tenacity.

How To Develop Resilience

Know that you can manage change.

View life's experiences as a learning curve.

Appreciate that change comes armed with Volatility, Uncertainty, Complexity and Ambiguity.

Consider all possibilities to handle the situation at hand.

Draw on or develop the Value and/or Strength of adaptability.

Believe you can cope with the situation you find yourself in.

View setbacks as opportunities from which to grow.

Don't jump to conclusions.

Live by and believe in the FEAR acronym – Face Everything And Rise.

Know it's OK not to succeed first time around.

Tell yourself that for every No you are closer to a Yes.

Be kind to yourself:

- *Ask for help when you need it.*
- *Pick yourself up, dust yourself down and continue.*
- *Laugh at yourself.*
- *Surround yourself with people you like, those who make you feel good and who make you laugh.*
- *Sleep.*
- *Go for walks.*
- *Take breaks.*
- *Get Leggy with your negative, pessimistic and gloomy Thoughts and Emotions.*
- *Reward yourself along the journey, not just at your destination.*

Observe and copy others who demonstrate resilience.

Ask others how they develop resilience.

As a reminder, in *Chapters One, Five, Six* and *Eight*, Anna, Pauline and I demonstrated *resilience* in the following ways:

Anna ...

- Stepped out of her comfort zone, joining networking events and hobby groups to make friends.
- Persisted in keeping Abigail alive in her life. She listened to music they both liked and placed photos around her home.
- Did things she enjoyed, including going out in her rowing boat.

I ...

- Was determined to swim like a professional.
- With the help of my neighbour, mastered the Dutch ticket and locker system at the local swimming baths.
- Repeatedly looked for opportunities to improve my physical, emotional and psychological health.

Pauline ...

- Was determined to find another place to live when trust between her and her landlord was broken.

- Discovered that employment opportunities opened up after learning Dutch and improving her English language skills.
- Remained determined to support her dying father and do the best for her mum despite the difficulties in their relationships.
- Faced Everything And Rose through the difficult months leading to the death of both her parents.

WILLINGNESS TO LEARN

"Learning is a weightless treasure you can always carry easily."
Chinese proverb

Definition

Keen to acquire knowledge and develop new and existing skills and Strengths.

Synonyms

Being open; Curiosity; Inquisitiveness.

How To Develop a Willingness to Learn

Identify and utilise your preferred learning style. Do you learn best by doing, by reading and studying, by reflecting, by questioning, by observing, or through a combination of these?

Be open to discovering new ways to grow and develop.

- *Investigate, research and gather information on subjects of interest.*
- *Do new things.*
- *Review mistakes to identify what can be done differently next time.*
- *Seek feedback from others.*
- *Look to become an expert in areas that excite and motivate you.*

Network and connect with others.

- *Listen.*
- *Observe.*
- *Ask questions.*

Be committed to continuous self-improvement:

- *Add to your existing knowledge.*
- *Seek alternative ways of doing things, not just the tried and tested.*
- *Appreciate that developing new skills helps to manage change.*
- *Develop your existing Values and Strengths.*

- *Develop new Values and Strengths.*
- *Learn from your mistakes by reflecting and evaluating.*
- *View mistakes as opportunities from which to learn and grow.*
- *Look at which of your Strengths compensate for your Weaknesses.*
- *Look to others for support in your areas of Weakness.*

Observe and copy others who are good at learning.

Ask others how they learn.

As a reminder, in *Chapters Five, Eight* and *Nine*, Hortense and Matilde demonstrated a *willingness to learn* in the following ways:

Hortense and Matilde learned the language and its nuances to adapt to their host countries.

Hortense ...
- Sought answers to why the locals did what they did.
- Sought to understand the *why* behind locals' behaviours, focusing on where the emphasis is placed in the language.
- Spoke with friends and joined networking groups in order to understand the behaviours of locals.
- Researched the economy and educational requirements of several countries.
- Was willing to work in the public sector, a sector in which she had little experience.
- Realised that finding work of a similar status to what she'd had in her home country can take years.

Matilde ...
- Learned that language nuances can be difficult to decipher.
- Realised that talking with strangers can help ease feelings of loneliness.
- Realised how sharing caring responsibilities with her brother was a welcome distraction from the stressful situation they were both in.
- Attended check-up appointments with her mum to gain a clear understanding of her mum's healing journey.

SWIMMING LESSON THIRTEEN
Developing Your Values and Strengths

In Swimming Lesson Thirteen, you are being tasked with identifying the extent to which the Values and Strengths highlighted in Chapter Five are yours. You will identify ways in which to develop these Values and Strengths as your own and identify compensatory Values and Strengths for those that are your weaknesses.

The lesson is in five Parts. Complete all five. It may take longer than the suggested timeframes, and that's OK.

PART ONE

Plot each of the following Values and Strengths in the competence and confidence matrix. Be honest with yourself. Ask yourself, *Am I good at this?* (Competence) and *Do I enjoy this?* (Confidence)

Adaptability	Observation Skills
Connections	Perseverance
Courage	Pragmatism
Humour	Questioning Skills
Integrity	Resilience
Listening Skills	Willingness to Learn

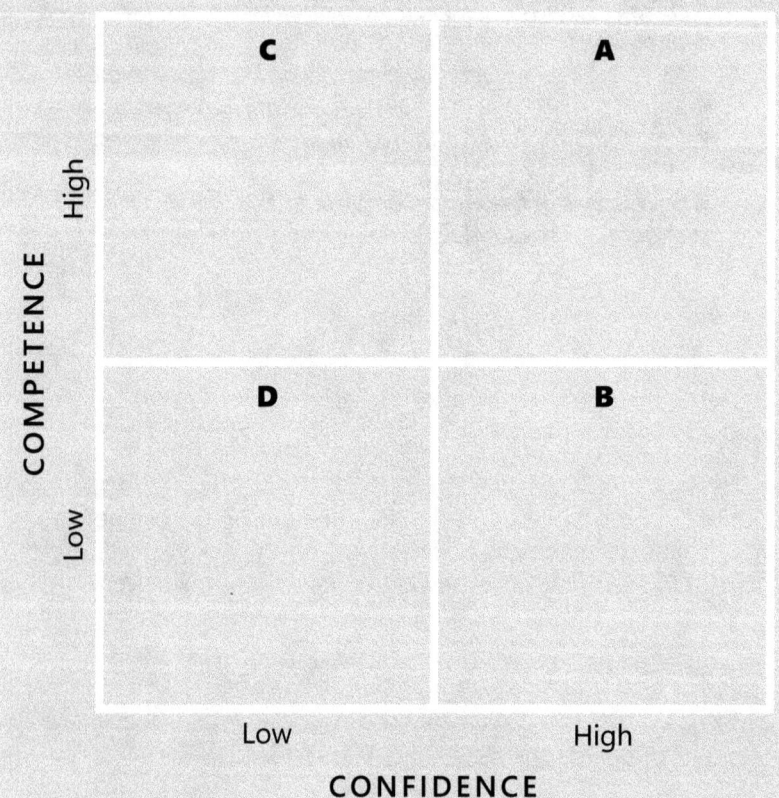

PART TWO

List below the Values and Strengths you placed in box A (high competence and high confidence). Next to each Value and Strength, detail ways you intend to develop these further. Refer to the suggestions earlier in this chapter for ideas. Set a date to practise each Value and Strength.

After practising, come back and detail what you learned and what you intend to do to further develop your competence and confidence.

Value/Strength	I commit to ...	Date

What I have learned from practising these Values and Strengths

What I will do to further develop my competence and confidence

PART THREE

List below the Values and Strengths you placed in box B (high confidence and low competence). Next to each Value and Strength, detail ways in which you can increase your competence. Refer to the suggestions earlier in this chapter for ideas. Set a date to practise each Value and Strength.

After practising, come back and detail what you learned and what you intend to do to further improve your competence.

Value/Strength	I commit to ...	Date

What I have learned from practising these Values and Strengths

What I will do to further improve my competence

PART FOUR

List below the Values and Strengths you placed in box C (high competence and low confidence). Next to each Value and Strength, detail ways in which you can increase your confidence. Refer to the suggestions earlier in this chapter for ideas. Set a date to practise each Value and Strength.

After practising, come back and detail what you learned and what you intend to do to further increase your confidence.

Value/Strength	I commit to ...	Date

What I have learned from practising these Values and Strengths

What I will do to further increase my confidence

PART FIVE

List below the Values and Strengths located in box D (low competence and low confidence). These are your Weaknesses. Next to each Weakness, identify which of your own Values and Strengths realised in *Swimming Lessons Five* and *Six* could compensate for these and how.

Weakness	Compensatory Value or Strength and How

Chapter Summary

In this chapter you learned ...

- How to master swimming strokes.
- The importance of defining and developing Values and Strengths.
- How to develop the Values and Strengths of adaptability, connections, courage, humour, integrity, listening skills, observation skills, perseverance, pragmatism, questioning skills, resilience and willingness to learn.
- Whether adaptability, connections, courage, humour, integrity, listening skills, observation skills, perseverance, pragmatism, questioning skills, resilience, and willingness to learn are any of your Weaknesses and, if so, how some of your own Values and Strengths may compensate for these.

In this chapter you have completed one Swimming Lesson.

Congratulate yourself. You've earned your tenth swimming medal.

Useful Resources

- Read *Courage*. Osho. 1999. St Martin's Press.
- Read *Developing Resilience*. Michael Neenan. 2018. Routledge.
- Read *Endurance*. Alfred Lansing. 2003. Weidenfeld and Nicolson.
- Read *Focus*. Jurgen Wolff. 2008. Pearson Education Limited.
- Read *How to Be Funny in Social Situations*. Rui Oliveira. 2021. Independently Published.
- Read *Persuasion, Chapter Two*, Being a Good Listener, *Chapter Four*, Mind Your Body Language and *Chapter Six*, Make Words Work for You – The Power of Psycholinguistics. James Borg. 2007. Pearson Education Limited.
- Read *The Courage Map*. Franziska Iseli. 2020. TCK Publishing.

A Ripple of Laughter

Why do some fish swim at the bottom of the ocean?
Because they dropped out of school.

CHAPTER ELEVEN

Be a Shellfish? Nope, Be Selfish

"To be what we are, and to become what we are capable of becoming, is the only end in life."

Robert Louis Stevenson
Scottish novelist, poet, essayist and travel writer

Self-Leadership

In *One Minute for Myself*, author Spencer Johnson states, "The greatest reason for outer success – at work and in life – is inner success."

But what exactly is inner success?

Inner success is about being true to who you are – your authentic self. When you live authentically, you are living your Values, utilising your Strengths, recognising and understanding your Thoughts and Emotions and following your intuition and gut feelings. Conversely, when you are not acting in alignment with your authentic self, you'll find you conform to things that don't sit comfortably with you, and you may subsequently play a role you believe others are expecting you to play.

Being your authentic self is essential, and no more so than when you live abroad. However, at times, this isn't easy.

In *Chapter Five*, Laura explained how she felt she was living on parallel tracks, doing her utmost to be her authentic self on one track while adapting to the differences between her host and home country on the other. When the tracks crossed, she experienced culture shock. Her authentic self was being tested. This will happen to you too.

So, how do you remain true to who you are when being repeatedly challenged by differences between your home and host countries? The answer lies in being 'selfish', looking at what I refer to as the A, B and C of Self: Self-**A**wareness, Self-**B**elief and Self-**C**onfidence. When you have Self-Awareness, the belief you have in yourself increases, and when you have Self-Belief, your Self-Confidence increases. You become the successful leader of your life abroad, better equipped to handle the Volatility, Uncertainty, Complexity and Ambiguity of stressful situations, whatever they may be.

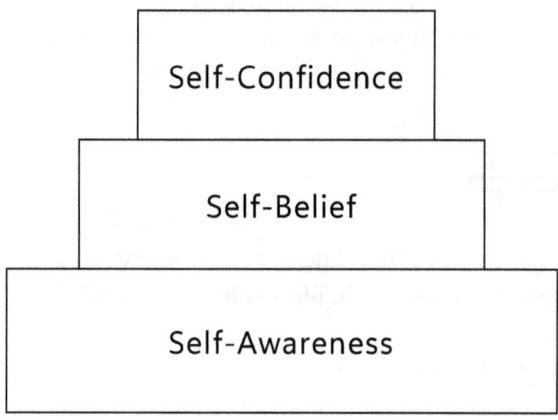

Fig. 11.1 – Self-Leadership Building Blocks

Let's take a moment to look at these in turn.

Self-Awareness – I Am ...

According to Aristotle, "Knowing yourself is the beginning of all wisdom." When you know yourself, you are conscious of what makes you you, and you understand why you do what you do. You are Self-Aware. The voice in your head says *I am adaptable. I am resilient. I am ...* all those qualities that make you, you.

To develop Self-Awareness:

- Focus on the present moment and tune in to your senses. What do you see, hear, feel, smell, taste and sense? Say out loud what you are aware of. For example, I see the smile on his face; I hear rain tapping against the window; I feel a flutter of excitement in my belly; I smell lavender in the air.
- Be conscious of your Thoughts and Emotions.
- Listen to your inner voice.
- Be aware of how you speak to yourself.
- Be aware of your behaviours and communication style.
- Laugh at yourself, including your faults and mistakes.
- Be curious to learn more about who you are.
- Know your Values and Strengths.
- Know what comes naturally to you.
- Know what's important to you.

Developing Self-Awareness – My Story

For years I've used several tools designed to identify behavioural preferences, communication styles, emotional intelligence facets, motivational traits, Strengths and Values. While these have helped me increase my own Self-Awareness, they did so only at surface level. When I began the somatic healing journey following the second cancer diagnosis, I learned the importance of observing and listening to my Thoughts as well as sitting with my Emotions and letting them flow through me. I learned more about who I was *and* why I was who I was. I became Self-Aware at a much deeper level.

Understanding my Thoughts and Emotions unveiled how my Values and Strengths of *independence, continuous improvement, growth, service, and quality* had hindered my ability to ask for help and to know when to stop and rest. I had, for countless years, been driving myself into the ground. A workaholic, I had hardly ever set boundaries in my life and rarely said no to things I didn't enjoy.

> I was a people pleaser, putting others before myself. But, the healing journey put a stop to that. I now journal daily, document my Thoughts and Emotions, and assess where I can make further changes in my life to prevent over- and sometimes under-use of my Values and Strengths.

Self-Awareness matters. When you are Self-Aware your Self-Belief increases.

Self-Belief – I Can ...

Professional tennis player Novak Djokovic once said, "Everybody believes in something ... Most of all, we should believe in ourselves." When you see and value the best in yourself, you have Self-Belief, which in turn increases your chances of success in life. When you have Self-Belief, the voice in your head shouts, *I can do this.*

To develop your Self-Belief:

- Be yourself.
- Be Self-Aware.
- View change as an opportunity as opposed to a challenge.
- Know that you cannot change the circumstances you find yourself in, but you can change how you respond.
- Know that you *can* Face Everything And Rise.
- Know that if you believe you can, *you can.*
- Live your Values.
- Utilise your Strengths.
- Draw on your Strengths to compensate for your Weaknesses.
- Get Leggy with negative Thoughts and Emotions.
- Think positive Thoughts.
- Talk positively and purposefully to yourself.
- View mistakes as lessons from which to grow.
- Place trust in your abilities.

> ### Developing Self-Belief – My Story
>
> On a flight from the UK to the Netherlands in 2018, I chatted with a lady who had recently emigrated to the UK from the Far East. It was her first time living abroad. She was learning the language and believed she would achieve a reasonable level of English but would never be fluent. Her belief fascinated me. The perfectionist in me had always believed fluency in a second language was possible. But, culture shock, embedding itself in my Thoughts and Emotions, had made the reality of learning languages an uphill struggle.
>
> Achieving fluency in a second language had been too high an expectation to place on myself. This unrealistic belief needed to be toned down. I subsequently relaxed my Values and Strengths of *growth* and *quality* and am now content, knowing that when I'm speaking a language other than my mother tongue, I'm understood by others – and I, in the main, understand them. I no longer put pressure on myself to achieve perfection. I'm happy to leave that to the natives.

Self-Belief matters. When you believe in yourself you feel confident and when you are confident you believe in yourself.

Self-Confidence – I Am ... and I Can ...

Thomas Edison, the inventor of the lightbulb, once said, "If we did everything we were capable of, we would literally astound ourselves." Knowing and believing in yourself *and* embracing who you are boosts your confidence and ultimately leads to success. When confident, you are motivated to succeed. The voice in your head roars, *I AM adaptable and resilient and I CAN do this.* To develop your Self-Confidence:

- Be yourself.
- Be Self-Aware.
- Believe in yourself.

- Review your Values and Strengths regularly.
- Develop new Values and Strengths.
- Further develop your existing Values and Strengths.
- Seek ways to stretch your potential, including:
  - Tackling challenges head-on.
  - Connecting with others to build new relationships.
  - Expressing your views openly.
  - Mirroring others who are confident.
  - Seeking feedback from others to understand yourself better.
- Write affirmations and say these out loud. For example, "I am confident and I will succeed."
- Use your talents and abilities to achieve your goals.

Developing Self-Confidence – My Story

In 2013, demoralised and deflated by job application rejections from Norwegian employers, I repatriated to the UK. Living alone and in a job I disliked, my all-time low Self-Confidence dived lower. My World crumbled. Desperate to return home to be with Hans, I frantically sent out application after application to Norwegian employers. Nothing happened. Months later, after being able to get out of a long-term rental contract without financial penalty, I returned to Norway.

Within three weeks I received a job offer. Yes, the contract was temporary, and yes, the job took me back to the beginning of my career, but I didn't care.

For ten years, my determination and perseverance had fuelled my belief that one day I would succeed in securing a job in Norway. That day had arrived. My Self-Confidence received a well-overdue boost. It was now time to prove myself to a Norwegian employer. Drawing on my extensive knowledge and experience, my Self-Confidence was boosted further as I dealt with a range of international HR issues. Eight months later I was promoted to Global HR Manager.

Self-Confidence matters. When you are confident you feel comfortable with the uncomfortable. As the leader of your life, you navigate your way through life's challenges, viewing them as opportunities to learn and grow.

🏊 SWIMMING LESSON FOURTEEN
Get Selfish

In Swimming Lesson Fourteen, you will realise the extent to which you have Self-Awareness, Self-Belief and Self-Confidence and will identify how to develop these further. The lesson is in four parts. Complete all four. Complete parts one, two and three in consecutive days. Move to part four only when you have completed the previous three.

PART ONE

Day One – Journal when you noticed you were Self-Aware. What were you doing? What specifically were you aware of? Include your Thoughts, Emotions, Values and Strengths.

At the end of day one, answer ... On a scale of 1 to 10, how Self-Aware are you? (1 = not at all and 10 = fully)

Your answer:

PART TWO

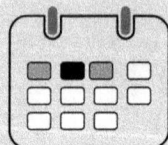

Day Two – Journal when you noticed you had Self-Belief. What were you doing? What specifically did you believe about yourself? Include your Thoughts, Emotions, Values and Strengths.

At the end of day two, answer ... On a scale of 1 to 10, how much Self-Belief do you have? (1 = not at all and 10 = fully)

Your answer:

PART THREE

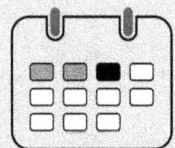

Day Three – Journal when you noticed you were Self-Confident. What were you doing? What specifically were you confident about? Include your Thoughts, Emotions, Values and Strengths.

At the end of day three, answer ... On a scale of 1 to 10, how Self-Confident are you? (1 = not at all and 10 = fully)

Your answer:

PART FOUR

Reflecting on your answers to Part One, Two and Three, write below how you intend to further develop your Self-Awareness, Self-Belief and Self-Confidence. Refer to the suggestions earlier in this chapter for ideas.

Reward Yourself

Rewards can be a great motivator when dealing with life's challenges.

What motivates us is a subject that has been researched for many years and from which several theories have been developed. These include Herzberg's two-factor theory of motivation, Maslow's hierarchy of needs, McGregor's X and Y theory and Skinner's reinforcement theory. Each theory highlights what motivates people, but from different perspectives. You may be motivated by extrinsic rewards such as money, gifts, certificates and recognition or by intrinsic rewards such as autonomy, having pride in what you do and learning something new. You may also be motivated by a combination of the two. There is no magic formula.

As the leader of your life abroad, you decide which rewards motivate you. What gives you a sense of satisfaction when you've completed a project or task? What keeps you going along the way? Like Nicole, you may have an evening in watching your favourite movies, digging into a box of your favourite chocolates or, like Hortense, have an evening out with friends.

If you get stuck on ways to reward yourself, here are some ideas:

- Take a day off.
- Go on a day trip.
- Eat out.
- Go to the cinema.
- Buy a new book.
- Buy your favourite flowers.
- Pamper yourself.
- Speak with a friend you haven't spoken with for a while.
- Give yourself a pat on the back.
- Buy something for yourself.
- Do something you enjoy that you've been putting off.
- Share what you've done with family and friends.

First You Sink and Then You Swim

Life brings wave upon wave of change, and dealing with these waves can be extremely demanding. Repeatedly bobbing up and down on Cultural Waves, navigating the differences between your home and host country *and* managing one if not more of life's most stressful situations, is undoubtedly challenging. Docking your authentic self at the nearest port and taking on board cultural norms, beliefs and Values that directly collide with your own, you may find yourself in floods of tears, feeling vulnerable and incompetent. You may no longer know who you are and where you belong.

Yet with these same challenges comes wave upon wave of opportunity. On a journey of discovery and exploration, you live somewhere that maybe you've never even visited, you develop friendships with people all over the world, and you embrace cultural norms, beliefs and Values that complement your own.

Change in life is a given. There is no escape. Laden with Volatility, Uncertainty, Complexity and Ambiguity, it turns Your World upside down and inside out. However, with the know-how and several tools and techniques designed to help you deal with change, maybe, just maybe, you have begun to view change as not so difficult after all. Get Leggy with negative Thoughts and Emotions, learn from the experiences of others, and realise and develop existing and new Values and Strengths. Increase your Self-Awareness, Self-Belief and Self-Confidence. And when you do these things, you turn Volatility, Uncertainty, Complexity and Ambiguity on their heads:

- Volatility becomes stability and security.
- Uncertainty converts to certainty and assurance.
- Complexity transforms into simplicity and ease.
- Ambiguity shifts to become clarity and straightforwardness.

How you previously viewed change has changed. Change *is* surmountable. The challenges and opportunities you encounter when living abroad are experiences from which you learn and grow and from which your life is enriched. You now appreciate you can survive life's most stressful situations when living abroad because you know for sure that first you sink and then you swim.

The Six Steps to Swimming Again

In *Sink Then Swim* I have shared several tools and techniques. Together they form your survival toolkit designed to enable you to survive life's most stressful situations when living abroad.

> ### THE SIX STEPS TO SWIMMING AGAIN
>
> 1. Get Leggy with your negative, pessimistic and gloomy Thoughts and Emotions.
>
> 2. Live your Values.
>
> 3. Utilise your Strengths.
>
> 4. Learn from the experiences of others.
>
> 5. Develop Existing and New Values and Strengths.
>
> 6. Have Self-Awareness, Self-Belief and Self-Confidence. Be the successful leader of your life abroad.

🏊 SWIMMING LESSON FIFTEEN
The Six Steps to Swimming Again

In Swimming Lesson Fifteen, you are being asked to commit to The Six Steps to Swimming Again.

List one thing you intend to do during the next month for each of The Six Steps to Swimming Again.

Steps	I intend to ...
1. Get Leggy	*For example:* stop and take a deep breath when I am sad and think a happy thought instead.
2. Live your Values	*For example:* build more rest time into my day. Sit and read or draw in my colouring book.

Steps	I intend to ...
3. Utilise your Strengths	*For example:* continue to utilise my Strength of service to compensate for my Weakness of being competitive.
4. Learn from the experiences of others	*For example:* read books written in Dutch to improve my language skills.
5. Develop Existing and New Values and Strengths	*For example:* laugh at myself and the circumstance I find myself in to ease pressure, stress and anxiety.

Steps	I intend to ...
6. Have Self-Awareness, Self-Belief and Self-Confidence. Become the successful leader of your life abroad	*For example:* stop when my confidence falters. Ask myself what the cause is and what to do to increase my confidence.

Revisit your answers regularly, asking, *What have I achieved and what will I commit to next?*

Chapter Summary

Be a Shellfish? Nope, Be Selfish
Sue's Final Comments

Life abroad is full of challenge *and* opportunity. Your new normal comprises a combination of disruption, chaos, unpredictability, excitement, fun and adventure. You experience wild whirlpools one minute and cascading waterfalls the next.

While you cannot control what happens in your life abroad and you may not have all the answers to deal with what's happening, you do now have the know-how and a survival toolkit to guide and support you along the way.

Whenever you feel like a fish out of water or are swimming against the tide, know that you first sink and then you swim. You can and will survive life's most stressful situations when living abroad.

In this chapter you learned ...

- The importance of being selfish.
- Inner success is achieved by being your authentic self.
- Inner success leads to outer success.
- You are your natural, authentic self, the successful leader of your life abroad when you are Self-Aware, have Self-Belief and are Self-Confident.
- Self-Awareness, Self-Belief and Self-Confidence matter.
- Rewards can motivate you to deal with life's challenges.
- Ways in which to reward yourself.
- Implementing your survival toolkit, The Six Steps to Swimming Again, will enable you to survive life's most stressful situations when living abroad.

In this chapter you have completed two Swimming Lessons.

Congratulate yourself. You've earned your eleventh swimming medal.

Useful Resources

- Listen and sing along to *Celebration*. Kool & the Gang. https://www.youtube.com/watch?v=cIg6odS-fA0
- Read 'Acceptance – Action for Happiness'. http://actionforhappiness.org/10-keys/acceptance
- Read *Atomic Habits*. James Clear. 2018. Random House Business Books.
- Read *Authentic: How to Be Yourself and Why it Matters*. Page 118, The domino effect of authenticity. Stephen Joseph. 2019. Piatkus books.
- Read *Awaken to Your True Self*. Andre Daniel. 2022. MetaHeal.
- Read *Becoming Your Best Possible Self*. Gerard Morgan. 2023. Orla Kelly Publishing.
- Read *Liquid Leadership*. Damian Hughes. 2007. Liquid Thinker. Self-published.

- Read *The Power of Now*. Eckhart Tolle. 2020. Yellow Kite.
- Read *What Motivates Me: Put Your Passions to Work*. Adrian Gostick and Chester Elton. 2014. The Culture Works Press.
- Watch *Motivational Theories Explained in 10 Minutes*. EPM. https://www.youtube.com/watch?v=woa2Qa8i80U&t=280s
- Watch *Self Awareness*. TalentSprout. https://www.youtube.com/watch?v=HIhEMk7CZ-A
- Watch *The Power Of The Present Moment – Living In The Now*. Fearless Soul. https://www.youtube.com/watch?v=Ci4Wg6MFcT4
- Watch *The Power of Self-Belief – Motivational Video*. Eddie Pinero. https://www.youtube.com/watch?v=I_mPoUWBMf4
- Watch *What is self-confidence. Think and Grow Rich*. https://www.youtube.com/watch?v=w4VpVbrtPZA
- Watch *When Was The Last Time You Celebrated?* Tony Robbins. https://www.youtube.com/watch?v=mCDW7I1HBpU
- Watch *3 tips to boost your confidence*. Ted-Ed. https://www.youtube.com/watch?v=l_NYrWqUR40
- Watch *15 Ways to Reward Yourself Without Spending a Lot*. Liv Positive. https://www.youtube.com/watch?v=9_J0m6E6xPU

A Ripple of Laughter

You made it to the end. You're shrimply the best. Congratulations.

SUE'S FINAL MESSAGE

"You can and will survive life's most stressful situations when living abroad. Embrace these challenges as opportunities from which to learn and grow, knowing that first you sink and then you swim."

BIBLIOGRAPHY

Bellingham, L. *There's Something I've Been Dying to Tell You*. 2014. London, UK. Coronet.

Burnett, B. and Evans, D. *Designing Your Work Life*. 2020. London, England. Penguin.

Clear, J. *Atomic Habits*. 2018. London, UK. Penguin Random House.

Elizur, D. and Sagie, A. 'Facets of Personal Values: A Structural Analysis of Life and Work Values'. 1999. *Applied Psychology: An International Review 48* (1).

Hayes, N. and Orrell, S. *Psychology: An Introduction*. 1987. New York, USA. Longman Inc.

Johnson, S. *One Minute for Myself*. 1985. New York, USA. Avon Books.

Lemieux, D. and Parker, A. *The Mobile Life*. 2013. The Hague, The Netherlands. XPat Media.

Linley, A. and Bateman, T. *The Strengths Profile Book*. 2018. Birmingham, England. Capp Press.

McNulty, Y. 'Til stress do us part: the causes and consequences of expatriate divorce'. 2015. *Journal of Global Mobility Vol. 3*, No. 2.

LePera, N. *How To Do The Work: Recognise Your Patterns, Heal From Your Past + Create Your Self*. 2021. New York, USA. HarperCollins.

Solomon, C.M. and Schell, M.S. *Managing Across Cultures: The Seven Keys to Doing Business with a Global Mindset*. 2009. USA. McGraw Hill.

Tolle, E. *The Power of Now.* 2020. London, Great Britain. Yellow Kite, Hodder & Stoughton Ltd.

Turner, K.A. *Radical Remission: Surviving Cancer Against All Odds.* 2014. New York. Harper Collins.

VUCA. Learn more here: https://usawc.libanswers.com/faq/84869

ACKNOWLEDGEMENTS

Writing a book doesn't magically happen overnight. Well, not in my case, anyway. Constantly thinking about messages I wanted to get across, and not being in the right frame of mind or well enough to write, has meant getting this book to publication has taken longer than I had hoped. Furthermore, and importantly, I'm acutely aware that *Sink Then Swim* would not be in your hands right now had it not been for several people to whom I now wish to express my heartfelt gratitude.

Research and interviews form an integral part of this book. I had the privilege of working with some wonderful people who kindly agreed to share their stories. You know who you are. I am indebted to you all. **Thank you**. Additionally, I am immensely grateful to those who agreed to be test readers. Your constructive feedback was priceless. *Thank you*. I also acknowledge the following for giving permission to quote: US Army War College for the *VUCA model* and Capp Press/Cappfinity for Alex Linley and Trudy Bateman's *The Strengths Profile Book*. **Thank you**.

I am highly appreciative to the Springtime and Summertime Team. Firstly, to Jack Scott for creating the striking book cover that totally hits the mark and for his tireless backstage management in getting the book to market. Next, Jo Parfitt for her guidance and encouragement during her How to Write a How-to Book course and thereafter as my book coach. Reading, reviewing and commenting on this book, chapter by chapter, line by line, word by word, I recognise was no small task. And last but not least, Paddy Hartnett for his outstanding proof-edit. Your attention to detail and constructive feedback was second to none. ***Thank you so much, Jack, Jo and Paddy.***

Further appreciation goes to Greta Solomon and Lisa Friedman. Your writing courses inspired me to write.

To my family and friends, ***thank you*** for being my cheerleaders.

Finally, to you, the reader. This book has been written with you in mind, to guide, support and encourage you while dealing with life's most stressful situations when living abroad. **Thank you** for choosing to read *Sink Then Swim*.

ABOUT THE AUTHOR

Sue Schoormans, nee Luford, was born in the United Kingdom and, at the time of writing, has lived abroad for twenty-two years. She has over twenty-five years' experience in Human Resources (HR).

Covering the full realm of HR, from hiring to firing, Sue's forte has always been within recruitment. Coupled with working in positions and organisations not right for her, she developed a keen interest in and passion for ensuring people work where they blossom and shine. After leaving the corporate world, becoming a career coach was a natural next step.

While studying for a master's degree in International HR and globalisation, she became a cross-cultural trainer. Merging her HR knowledge and experience with her intercultural knowledge and her living abroad experiences in the USA, Norway and the Netherlands, her understanding of compatibility broadened. Ensuring a level of compatibility between a person and their profession remained critically important, but now added to the mix was where a person was living – their host country. The person and their profession, the person and where they live – both are equally and critically important.

Sue supports and assists expats, immigrants, asylum seekers, refugees, international students and repatriates with their forthcoming emigration or repatriation and with the inevitable changes they encounter abroad and back home. Having personally been hit by wave after wave of change in her own life, beginning with her parents' divorce at just three years old and more recently being diagnosed with metastasised breast cancer, she draws on her life's experiences, enabling others to live their best life abroad. *Sink Then Swim* encompasses many of these experiences.

www.ingramcontent.com/pod-product-compliance
Lightning Source LLC
Chambersburg PA
CBHW051533020426
42333CB00016B/1914